D

Chess Endgames for Kids

Karsten Müller

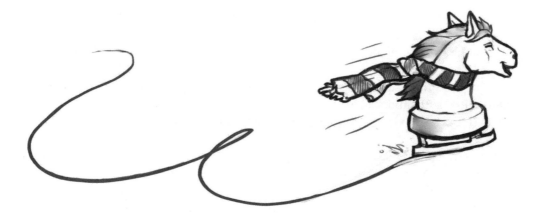

THE W-MANOEUVRE

First published in the UK by Gambit Publications Ltd 2015

ISBN-13: 978-1-910093-61-0
ISBN-10: 1-910093-61-0

DISTRIBUTION:
Worldwide (except USA): Central Books Ltd, 99 Wallis Rd, London E9 5LN, England.
Tel +44 (0)20 8986 4854 Fax +44 (0)20 8533 5821.
E-mail: orders@Centralbooks.com

Gambit Publications Ltd, 99 Wallis Rd, London E9 5LN, England.
E-mail: info@gambitbooks.com
Website (regularly updated): www.gambitbooks.com

Edited by Graham Burgess
Typeset by John Nunn
All illustrations by Shane D. Mercer
Printed in the USA by Bang Printing, Brainerd, Minnesota

10 9 8 7 6 5 4 3 2 1

Gambit Publications Ltd
Directors: Dr John Nunn GM, Murray Chandler GM, and Graham Burgess FM
German Editor: Petra Nunn WFM

Contents

PAWN RACE

Rook Endgames

Rooks and Minor Pieces

Queen Endgames

And Finally...

Introduction

This book is for every chess-player who has learned the rules, played some games and studied basic tactics, but knows very little about the endgame. It starts at the very beginning, with the basic mates, such as forcing checkmate with a queen or rook against a bare king. I go on to provide the essential endgame knowledge that you will need as you start to face more challenging opponents.

We shall be focusing on endgames where both sides have no more than a king, some pawns and one other piece. Studying the fundamental motifs is highly rewarding as endgame theory doesn't change rapidly, and this knowledge will be useful as long as you play chess; it will not get outdated like opening analysis. Endgame training also highlights the strong sides and limitations of all the pieces very clearly, which will help you in the other phases of the game too.

Unfortunately, simply reading this book is not sufficient. Endgame play requires practical skills, as well as theoretical knowledge. You should also solve the exercises and practice the key positions and techniques against a friend or a computer. Only then can you really be sure that you have mastered, e.g., how to checkmate with a rook, or that you know how to defend a standard rook ending.

I consider pawn endings and rook endings the most important endgame topics. Pawn endings form the basic foundation of endgame theory. Almost all other endings can lead to a pawn ending through an exchange of pieces, so it is very hard to assess 'higher' endgames without a knowledge of pawn endings. Pawn endgames also provide very good training in the calculation of long variations, since neither side has a wide choice of moves at their disposal. Rook endings are the ones that occur most often in practice, and there are many positions where knowing the right method or manoeuvre can make the difference between winning, drawing or losing.

Finally I want to thank Gambit Publications, and especially Graham Burgess for his superb editing work and help supplying the exercises.

Karsten Müller
Hamburg 2015

CHASING TWO HARES

Algebraic Notation

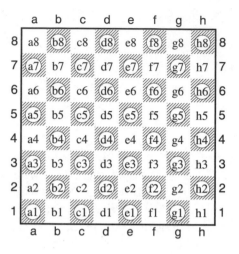

The chess notation used in this book is the simple, algebraic notation in use throughout the world. It can be learnt by anyone in just a few minutes.

As you can see from the chessboard above, the files are labelled a-h (going from left to right) and the ranks are labelled 1-8. This gives each square its own unique reference point. The pieces are described as follows:

Knight = ♞
Bishop = ♝
Rook = ♜
Queen = ♛
King = ♚

Pawns are not given a symbol. When they move, simply the *destination square* is given.

The following additional symbols are also used:

Check	=	+	Good move	=	!
Double Check	=	++	Bad move	=	?
Checkmate	=	#	Interesting idea	=	!?
Capture	=	x	Inaccurate move	=	?!
Castles kingside	=	0-0	Brilliant move	=	!!
Castles queenside	=	0-0-0	Disastrous move	=	??
See diagram 2 (etc.)	=	*(2)*			

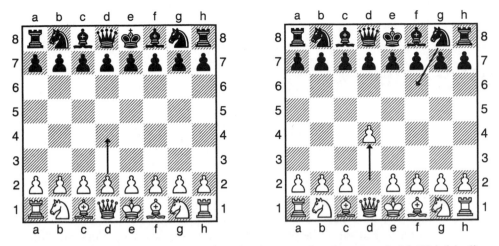

In the left-hand diagram above, White is about to play the move **1 d4**. The **1** indicates the move-number, and **d4** the destination square of the white pawn.

In the right-hand diagram, White's **1 d4** move is complete. Black is about to reply **1...♘f6** (moving his knight to the **f6-square** on his *first move*).

When a pawn promotes, the piece chosen is written immediately after the square where the pawn promotes. Thus e8♕ means that White moved his pawn to e8 and promoted to a queen.

In this book, there are many *game references*. This is a shorthand way of saying that a specific position and sequence of moves occurred in a game between two particular players. White's name is given first, followed by Black's name and the place and year where the game was played (e.g., Fischer-Spassky, Reykjavik 1972).

GEOMETRY OF THE CHESSBOARD

What's So Special About the Endgame?

A chess game generally has three stages: the opening, the middlegame and the endgame. In the opening, the players fight to bring out their pieces to good squares. In the middlegame they pursue a variety of plans while countering those of the opponent. They might attack the enemy king or simply try to dominate the position. In the middlegame, the king needs to be carefully protected, and every move is precious. However, once there have been many piece exchanges, we reach an endgame. How does this differ from a middlegame? Why do chess-players even make a distinction between the two? Mating attacks and sacrifices are still possible in the endgame, and the right to move can still be precious, but there are some major differences too. Firstly, the battle often centres around the fight to promote pawns, while long-term planning and lengthy calculation become more important. There are two other specific factors that must be noted:

The King
The role of the king changes completely in the endgame. In the middlegame it should usually be tucked away behind a solid wall of pawns. Due to the reduced firepower in the endgame, the king can play an active role instead. Indeed, not just *can* but *must*. If you don't use your king but the opponent uses his king, then you will be fighting with one piece less. The king is well suited to blockade enemy pawns and support its own pawns. It can also cause havoc by invading the enemy position, attacking pawns and pieces, and even join in a mating attack on his opposite number! So when you feel you have reached an endgame, be sure to include your king in your active plans, as soon as it is safe to do so.

The Right to Move – or is it a Burden?
In the opening and middlegame, the right to move is all-important. Sometimes it is worth sacrificing material just to gain time to play one extra move. That can also be true in the endgame, but there is another side to the coin. For a defender whose pieces and pawns are already on their best squares, the fact that he *has to* move can cause his downfall, as it forces him to move a piece away from its best square or to make a fatal pawn weakness. Experienced endgame players use this to their advantage, and base their plans around it. The name for this situation – where the right to move becomes an unpleasant burden – is **zugzwang**. This German word may be difficult to pronounce for many English speakers, but you'll soon be using the idea in your own games – and may already have done so – even if you can't quite get your tongue around the word itself.

Zugzwang can prove more powerful than direct threats and may even be the only way to win. Consider the following position:

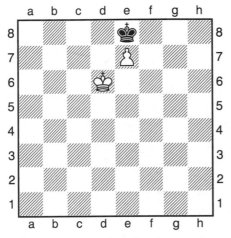

This is one of the simplest endgames and also one of the most important. Can White win? Not if it is his turn to move, as 1 ♔e6 is stalemate, and otherwise he must move his king away and Black can then take the pawn on e7. But if it is Black's turn to move, he must play 1...♔f7. White replies 2 ♔d7 and next move 3 e8♕, when he has a whole extra queen, with an easy win. Black was in zugzwang! If he could

BISHOP AND WRONG ROOK'S PAWN

simply 'pass' and leave his king on e8, White would have no way to win. But the rules of chess don't allow that. For more details, see Lesson 7.

The next example underlines the importance of zugzwang in the endgame.

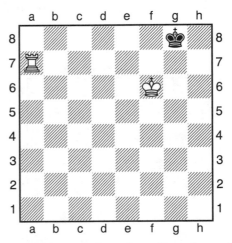

White is a whole rook up. Does he really need to use something as subtle as zugzwang to win? In fact, he docs. White could threaten mate by playing 1 ♔g6, but Black can reply 1...♔f8, parrying the threat of 2 ♖a8#. But if White plays a waiting move, such as 1 ♖b7, then Black has to make a move; he would like to 'pass' but he can't. 1...♔f8 allows instant mate by 2 ♖b8#, while 1...♔h8 is met by 2 ♔g6 and mate next move by 3 ♖b8#. We look at the ending of king and rook vs king in more detail in Lessons 3 and 4.

But zugzwang also has another side: what if *both* sides' pieces are in their best positions, so whoever is to move would be in zugzwang? This is called **mutual zugzwang**, and near such positions great accuracy is required, since you want to reach the key position with the opponent to move, rather than yourself. This might sound like a highly advanced concept, but it crops up in some of the most basic endgames. In fact, we have already seen it in our king and pawn vs king example (White to play could only draw; Black to play lost). Here is an even more dramatic example:

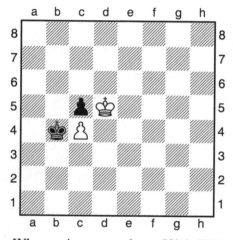

Whoever is to move *loses*. If it is White's turn to move, he can't take the c5-pawn and must move away, allowing Black to take the pawn on c4 and then promote his own pawn. One of the exercises at the end of the book is based on this idea, so please make a mental note of it. This and similar ideas also crop up quite often in practice.

Another theme we see several times in this book is the **fortress**. This is a position where one side has what would normally be an overwhelming advantage, but has no way to make progress. This is typically because all roads into the enemy position are blocked or because of stalemate ideas.

Here is one of the best-known:

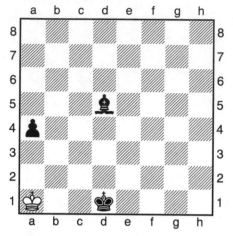

Black has an extra bishop and pawn, but there is no way he can remove the white king from the a1-corner. All he can do is give stalemate; e.g., 1...a3 2 ♔b1 a2+ 3 ♔a1 ♔d2 4 ♔b2 ♔d3 5 ♔a1 ♔c2 stalemate. The bishop can never control the a1-square because it only moves on light squares. See Lesson 24.

OUTSIDE PASSED PAWN

Here is a more surprising fortress:

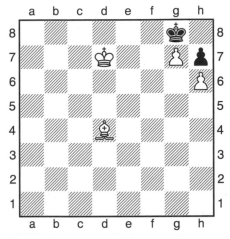

White is again a bishop and pawn up, but this time his bishop controls the corner square and he has a powerful-looking g7-pawn. But if the white king moves any closer it is stalemate, and giving up the g-pawn (e.g., 1 ♗c3 ♔f7 2 g8♕+ ♔xg8 3 ♔e6 ♔f8 4 ♗g7+ ♔g8) changes little.

We end with an example of the king as a strong attacking piece, which also shows

that material sacrifices are important in endgames:

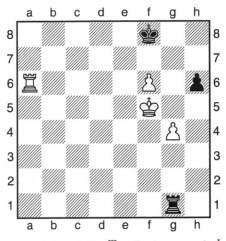

1 g5!? hxg5 (1...♖xg5+ loses to 2 ♔e6 ♔g8 3 ♖a8+ ♔h7 4 f7) 2 ♔g6.

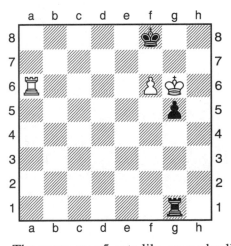

The pawn on g5 acts like an umbrella as it shelters the attacking king from the rain of rook checks (with the g5-pawn removed from the board, the position would be drawn). After 2...♖e1 3 ♖a8+ ♖e8 4 ♖xe8+ ♔xe8 5 ♔g7 g4 6 f7+ ♔d7 7 f8♕ g3 8 ♕f3 White wins; see Endgame Lesson 1 for the mate with king and queen.

Mate with the Queen

Throw a rope around the king, but beware of stalemate

This is a procedure you should be able to master even in your sleep. The attacker should mate in at most 10 moves and the only real hurdle is a possible stalemate, if the king and queen attack too clumsily. So you:

1) Advance your king.

2) Restrict the defending king with your queen, like throwing a rope along a file or rank.

3) Bring your king so close that the queen can give check and throw the rope again to force a cut-off further down the board. This goes on until Phase 4 is reached.

4) When the defending king is restricted to the edge of the board, it is time to give mate.

5) Be careful not to stalemate the defending king by tightening the rope too much.

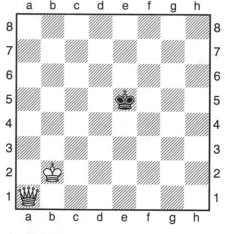

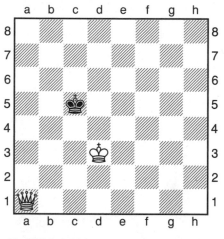

1) White to move

This is a relatively bad starting position, but White still mates quickly: 1 ♔c3 (the slower piece, the king, advances first) 1...♔d5 2 ♔d3 ♔c5 *(2)*.

2) White to move

Phase 1 is completed. Now the queen can give check to cut Black's king off. 3 ♕a5+ ('throwing the rope' with 3 ♕a4 also works as a way to restrict the king) 3...♔d6 *(3)*.

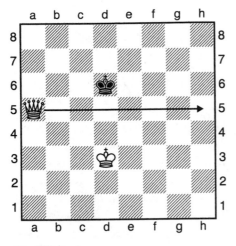

3) White to move

Now comes Phase 3. At the moment the queen cannot throw the rope directly again, so White's king moves in closer: 4 ♔d4 ♚e6 5 ♕g5 ♚d6 *(4)*.

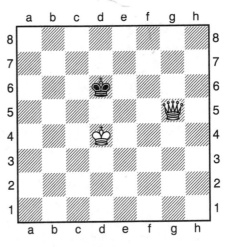

4) White to move

The pattern now repeats itself: Black is cut off further and further down the board. 6 ♕f6+ ♚d7 7 ♔d5 (the rope is on the sixth rank so the king moves closer) 7...♚e8 *(5)*.

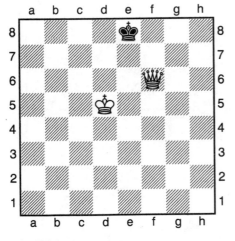

5) White to move

We have reached the dangerous transition point from Phase 3 to 4 in the process. 8 ♕g7 (but not 8 ♔e6?? stalemate) 8...♚d8 *(6)*.

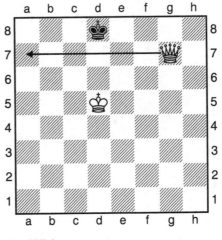

6) White to move

Now comes the final mating phase as the uncrossable rope is on the seventh rank: 9 ♔d6 ♚e8 (9...♚c8 10 ♕c7#) 10 ♕e7#.

2

Mate with Two Rooks

The lawn mower comes closer and closer

In contrast to the queen, two rooks do not need the help of the attacking king. They can force mate alone and the procedure is very easy and systematic. One rook cuts the defending king off along a file or rank from a distance. The other rook then checks on the file or rank where the defending king is, also from a distance. Together they are like a powerful lawn mover closing in on the king: he can run, but he can't hide. Once he is forced to the edge of the board, it will be mate. Just make sure that you move the rooks away from the defending king when he attacks one of them. That said, there is some margin for error here: the attacker can even blunder one rook and still win with the remaining one (see Lessons 3 and 4), though I certainly don't recommend this!

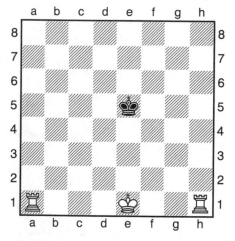

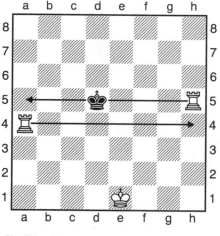

1) White to move

The first rook throws a rope along the fourth rank: 1 ♖a4 ♚d5 (1...♚f5 2 ♖h5+ is similar) 2 ♖h5+ *(2)*.

2) Black to move

The second rook joins White's attack. 2...♚c6 3 ♖a6+ (the pattern repeats itself and the king is forced back further and further) 3...♚b7 *(3)*.

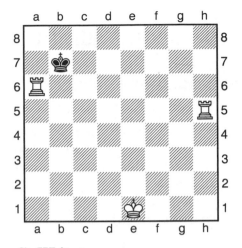

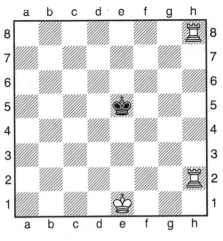

3) White to move

Now the rook must move into the distance. After 4 ♖g6 ♔c7 the final phase has come: 5 ♖h7+ ♔d8 6 ♖g8#.

4) White to move

You can mate in just the same way by using the rooks on files rather than ranks. The first rooks throws the rope: 1 ♖f2 ♔e6 2 ♖e8+ (the second rook joins the attack) 2...♔d7 (5).

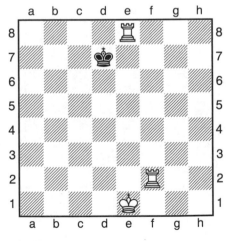

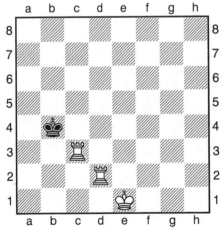

5) White to move

Now the rook must move into the distance: 3 ♖e3 ♔d6 4 ♖d2+ (the cut-off pattern repeats itself) 4...♔c5 5 ♖c3+ ♔b4 (6).

6) White to move

The rook is again too close: 6 ♖c8 ♔b3 7 ♖d7 (the second rook is also too close) 7...♔b4 8 ♖b7+ ♔a5 9 ♖a8#.

Mate with the Rook: Method 1

Make those rectangle prisons smaller and smaller

With one rook against a bare king, the attacker needs 16 moves to mate from the least favourable starting position, assuming best play by both sides. In this lesson and the next, I shall be presenting two systematic techniques to force mate. Neither method represents 'optimal' play in terms of forcing the quickest possible mate, but they are both easy to understand and can be done very quickly, with a little practice. Note that, whatever method he adopts, the attacker needs to use zugzwang in order to win, emphasizing the huge importance of this endgame weapon.

In this lesson, we examine the 'rectangle prison' technique:
1) Bring the king closer.
2) Limit the defending king to a rectangle with the rook.
3) Make the rectangle smaller and smaller until the defending king is at the edge of the board.
4) Force checkmate near a corner of the board.

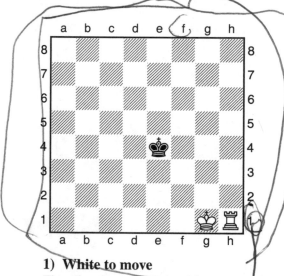

1) White to move
First the slower-moving king moves in as close as possible: 1 ♔f2 ♚f4 2 ♖h4+ ♚e5 3 ♔e3 ♚d5 4 ♖e4 *(2)*.

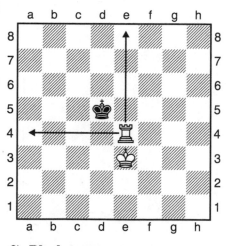

2) Black to move
Now the rook has confined the king to the rectangle prison a5-d5-d8-a8: 4...♚c5 5 ♖d4 (the rectangle is getting smaller) 5...♚c6 6 ♔e4 ♚c5 7 ♔e5 ♚c6 *(3)*.

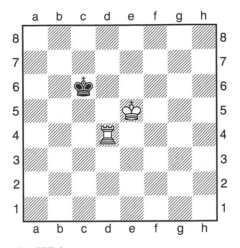

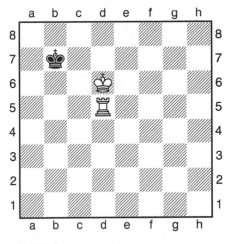

3) White to move

The rectangle gets smaller and smaller: 8 ♖d5 ♚b6 (8...♚c7 is met by 9 ♖d6) 9 ♚d6 ♚b7 *(4)*.

4) White to move

Now Phase 4 starts, where zugzwang plays a crucial role. Without the obligation to move for the defender, the attacker couldn't win – in sharp contrast to the mate with the queen. 10 ♖b5+ *(5)*.

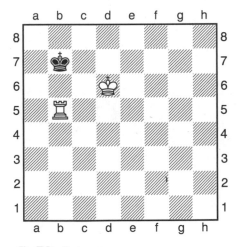

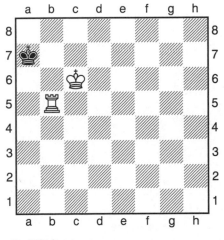

5) Black to move

10...♚a6 (10...♚c8 11 ♖b6 is zugzwang: 11...♚d8 12 ♖b8#) 11 ♚c6 ♚a7 *(6)*.

6) White to move

Now comes the end of the mating procedure. After 12 ♖b6 ♚a8 the rectangle has only two squares and should not be made smaller! 13 ♚c7 ♚a7 14 ♖c6 (zugzwang) 14...♚a8 15 ♖a6#.

17

ENDGAME LESSON 4   Mate with the Rook: Method 2

The rook can throw the rope just like the queen

The second technique for mating with one rook against a bare king is similar to the mating procedure with the queen. The rook needs more moves of course as the defending king can attack the rook. The rook also requires the help of the powerful endgame weapon zugzwang. This mating technique is as follows:

1) Bring the slower-moving king closer to the enemy king.

2) Cut the king off by throwing a rope along a file or rank.

3) When the kings are directly opposite each other on either side of the 'rope' (which you force by using zugzwang and the edge of the board), give a check to force the defender further back.

4) Repeat the procedure until the defending king is at the edge of the board and the next check is also mate.

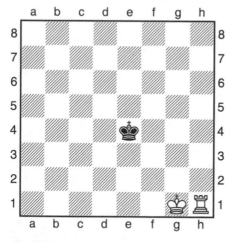

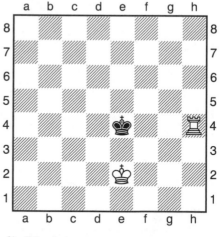

1) White to move

First the king moves closer: 1 ♔f2 ♚d4 2 ♔e2 ♚e4 (after 2...♚c4 3 ♔e3 ♚d5 the rook throws the rope along the fourth rank with 4 ♖h4) 3 ♖h4+ *(2)*.

2) Black to move

When the kings face each other, the rook can give check directly. 3...♚e5 4 ♔e3 ♚d5 5 ♖g4 (the rook uses zugzwang; 5 ♔d3?! ♚e5 doesn't bring White closer to mate) 5...♚c5 6 ♔d3 *(3)*.

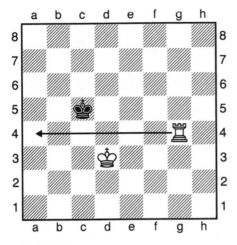

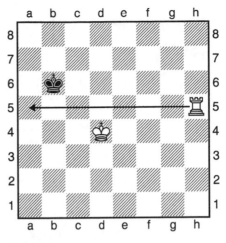

3) Black to move

The white king chases Black's king. 6...♔d5 (6...♔b5 7 ♔c3 ♔c5 8 ♖g5+ is similar) 7 ♖g5+ ♔e6 8 ♔e4 ♔d6 9 ♖h5 ♔c6 10 ♔d4 ♔b6 (4).

4) White to move

Again the king follows his black counterpart: 11 ♔c4 ♔c6 12 ♖h6+ ♔d7 13 ♔d5 ♔e7 (5).

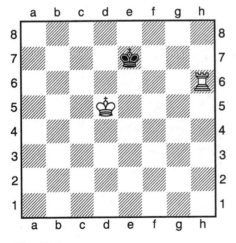

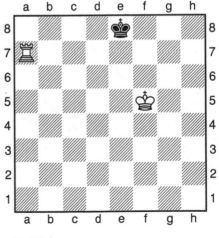

5) White to move

Now the rook can use the zugzwang technique while changing sides so that it is further from the defending king: 14 ♖a6 ♔f7 15 ♔e5 ♔g7 16 ♔f5 ♔f7 17 ♖a7+ ♔e8 (6).

6) White to move

Now comes the final mating phase: 18 ♔e6 ♔d8 (18...♔f8 19 ♖b7 is similar) 19 ♖h7 ♔c8 20 ♔d6 ♔b8 21 ♔c6 ♔a8 22 ♔b6 ♔b8 23 ♖h8#.

ENDGAME LESSON **5**   Mate with Two Bishops

Shoulder-to-shoulder, they imprison the king diagonally

Two bishops are more powerful than a rook, but they actually need longer to mate: 19 moves from the least favourable starting position. The procedure is not too complex, but slightly tricky to master, as three pieces need to be coordinated:

1) Cut the king off in a prison zone with the bishops working on parallel diagonals.
2) Move the king in closer and force the defending king back.
3) Make the prison zone smaller with the bishops.
4) Give mate once the defending king is near a corner.

Of course, we are assuming that the bishops move on different-coloured squares; two same-coloured bishops only occur extremely rarely (you have to promote a pawn to a bishop!), and cannot give mate.

This ends our discussion of the basic mates. The difficult mate with bishop and knight is dealt with in Lessons 49 and 50. Two knights cannot force mate against a bare king.

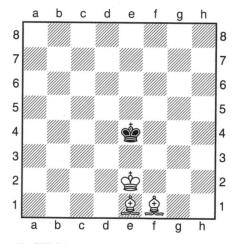

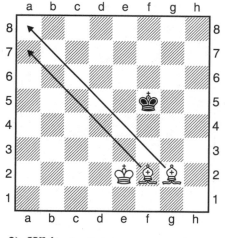

1) White to move

1 ♗f2 ♚e5 2 ♗g2 (the bishops stands shoulder-to-shoulder and limit the black king to the area around the north-east corner) 2...♚f5 *(2)*.

2) White to move

The second phase starts and the king moves in: 3 ♔f3 ♚e5 4 ♔g4 (Black's king must now retreat due to zugzwang) 4...♚e6 *(3)*.

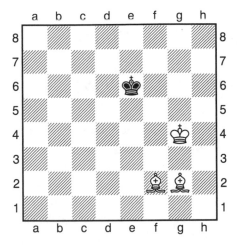

3) White to move

Now the bishops make Black's prison smaller: 5 ♗g3 ♚f6 (5...♚d7 is met by 6 ♗b7, closing the prison door) 6 ♗b7 ♚e6 *(4)*.

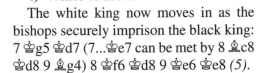

4) White to move

The white king now moves in as the bishops securely imprison the black king: 7 ♚g5 ♚d7 (7...♚e7 can be met by 8 ♗c8 ♚d8 9 ♗g4) 8 ♚f6 ♚d8 9 ♚e6 ♚e8 *(5)*.

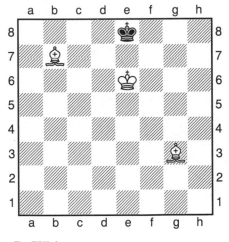

5) White to move

The mating phase now starts as Black's king can be forced into the north-east corner: 10 ♗c7 ♚f8 11 ♚f6 ♚e8 12 ♗c6+ ♚f8 *(6)*.

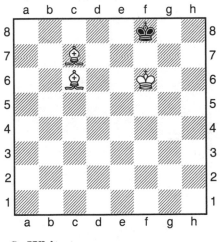

6) White to move

The rest is more or less clear: 13 ♗d6+ ♚g8 14 ♚g6 ♚h8 15 ♗e7 (not, of course, 15 ♗d5?? stalemate) 15...♚g8 16 ♗d5+ ♚h8 17 ♗f6#.

The Rule of the Square

Draw the diagonal to draw the conclusion

Pawn endings form the foundation of all other endgame skills, and the most fundamental pawn ending is king and pawn vs king. With some knowledge and practice, you should be able to assess all positions of this type perfectly, and to be able to work out the best moves. We'll start with positions where the attacking king cannot support his passed pawn, and it is a straight race between the pawn and the defending king. You *can* work this out by standard analysis ("I go there, he goes there..."), but the **rule of the square** is a useful shortcut. Let's assume the defender is to move. Then:

1) Draw a diagonal line from the passed pawn to its eighth rank and complete it to make a square.

2) If the defending king can move into the square, then it can stop the pawn; otherwise the passed pawn will queen.

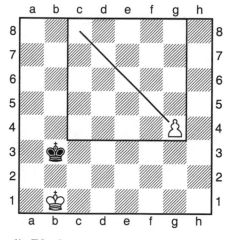

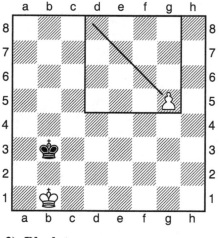

1) Black to move

Black's king can move into the square of the passed pawn (as marked in the diagram) with 1...♚c4 2 g5 ♚d5 3 g6 ♚e6 4 g7 ♚f7 5 g8♕+ ♚xg8, drawing.

2) Black to move

With the white pawn one square further up the board, Black's king can't move into the square, and so White wins: 1...♚c4 2 g6 ♚d5 3 g7 ♚e6 4 g8♕+.

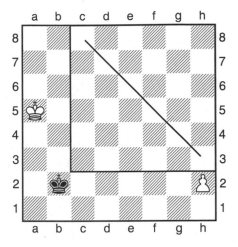

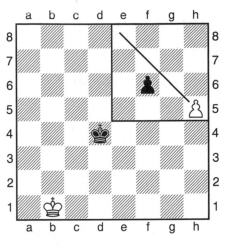

3) Black to move

For a pawn on its second rank, the square is drawn as if the pawn had advanced one square. Black's king moves into the square and stops the pawn: 1...♚c3 2 h4 ♚d4 3 h5 ♚e5 4 h6 ♚f6 5 h7 ♚g7.

4) Black to move

If a friendly pawn is in the way, matters can be different. Here Black's king can move into the square, but not stop the passed pawn: 1...♚e5 2 h6 ♚e6 3 h7 ♚f7 4 h8♛.

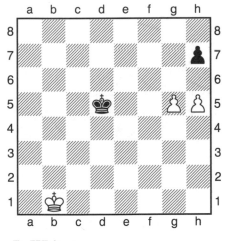

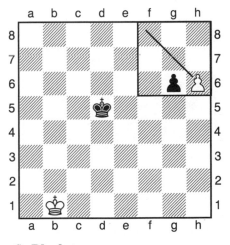

5) White to move

Sometimes a *breakthrough* is the best way to make use of a pawn-majority: 1 g6 hxg6 2 h6! *(6)* (2 hxg6? only draws). A pawn on h6 is further from the black king than one on g6.

6) Black to move

Black loses as the king cannot move into the square of the h6-pawn. With the white pawn instead on g6, the black king could enter its square with 2...♚e6!, drawing.

The Key Squares

Advance the king to a key square to unlock the gates

We now look at king and pawn vs king positions where the attacking king *can* support the pawn. There are two major cases to consider, since the defender has better drawing chances against a rook's pawn than when facing one of the other pawns. The winning chances are much higher with a pawn on the b- to g-file.

Usually the attacking king should advance first. If the attacking king can reach a **key square** of the pawn (which we'll define in diagrams 3, 4, 5 and 6) then the attacker always wins. Just advancing the pawn is usually insufficient as this strategy can easily lead to a draw due to our first position below.

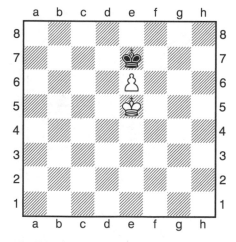

1) Black to move

Black draws with 1...♔e8! (1...♔f8? loses to 2 ♔f6 ♔e8 3 e7 ♔d7 4 ♔f7, and 1...♔d8? to 2 ♔d6) 2 ♔f6 ♔f8! *(2)*.

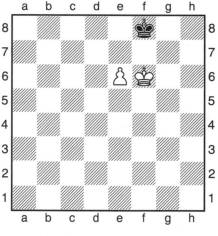

2) White to move

White cannot win as 3 e7+ ♔e8 4 ♔e6 is stalemate and 3 ♔e5 ♔e7 reaches the starting position again.

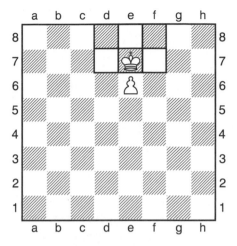

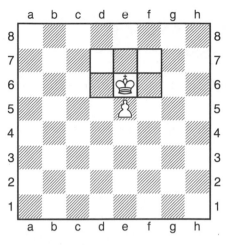

3) White/Black to move

So White's king should advance first to reach one of the marked squares. This wins with a pawn on e6 (as long as the pawn can't be taken immediately by Black's king, naturally).

4) White/Black to move

With a pawn on e5, the key squares for White's king are d7, e7, f7, d6, e6 and f6; White always wins if his king is on one of those squares. Again there are six key squares.

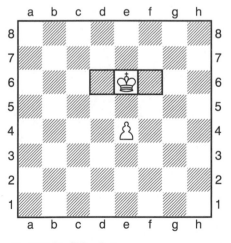

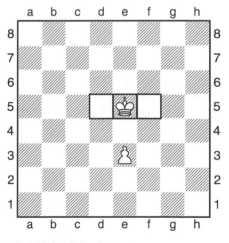

5) White/Black to move

With a pawn on e4 the key squares are only d6, e6 and f6. For example, if White's king is on e5 he may or may not be winning; it depends on where the black king is and who is to move.

6) White/Black to move

Here the key squares are d5, e5 and f5. A pawn that has crossed the middle of the board has six key squares; otherwise it has only three key squares. Every pawn move changes the key squares.

Opposition

Not only in the parliament is there opposition for the chess kings

This lesson explains the key-square configurations shown in Lesson 7 and introduces the concept of the *opposition*, which is the most important method in the fight for three adjacent key squares.

In the simplest case of the opposition, the kings face each other on the same file with one square in between them; the side *not* to move has the opposition as he can prevent the advance of the enemy king or force the advance of his own king. But note that this is just one form of the opposition – see Lesson 13 for a more general definition, and more complex cases.

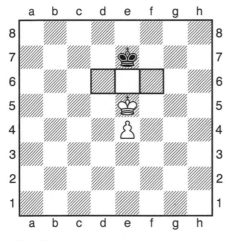

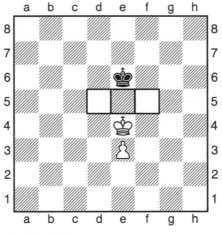

1) White to move

The three key squares are d6, e6 and f6. With White to move, Black has the opposition and draws: 1 ♔d5 ♚d7 and now 2 ♔e5 ♚e7 or 2 e5 ♚e7 3 e6 ♚e8!.

2) Black to move

With Black to move, White has the opposition and wins: 1...♚d6 2 ♔f5 (the king has reached a key square of the e3-pawn) 2...♚e7 *(3)*.

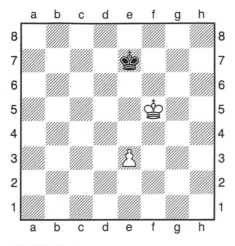

3) White to move

The king must take the opposition to advance further: 3 ♔e5! (the pawn move 3 e4? changes the key squares to d6, e6 and f6; Black defends them by 3...♚f7, taking the opposition) 3...♚f7 *(4)*.

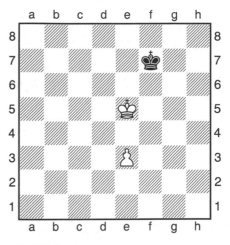

4) White to move

The king advances again: 4 ♔d6! (not 4 e4? ♚e7! – again Black defends by taking the opposition) 4...♚e8 5 e4 (now the pawn can move as the king has reached a key square) 5...♚d8 6 e5 *(5)*.

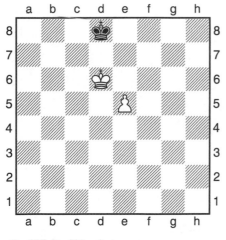

5) White/Black to move

The pawn can move again as d6 is also a key square for the e5-pawn. White also wins this position if he is to move by playing e6. This is the reason why the e5-pawn has six key squares. 6...♚e8 *(6)*.

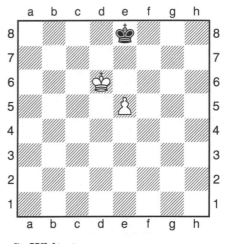

6) White to move

After 7 ♔e6 (7 e6? spoils everything due to 7...♚d8) 7...♚d8 8 ♔f7 the king has reached a key square for the e-pawn, whether it is on e5, e6 or e7. Thus the pawn can now safely advance and queen.

King and Rook's Pawn vs King

Always the same old two key squares

With a rook's pawn, the winning chances are much lower than with a pawn that is nearer the centre. There are only two key squares for the attacking king. With a white h-pawn the key squares are g8 and g7. So if the defender's king can reach the corner – or even the f8-square – then he draws as both key squares are protected.

So as before there may be a fight between the kings for the key squares. But this time a *bodycheck* is the main weapon. A bodycheck is less strictly defined than opposition. When one king takes one or more important squares from the other, this is a bodycheck.

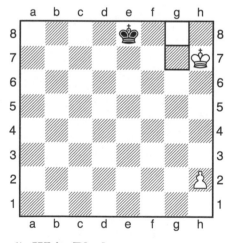

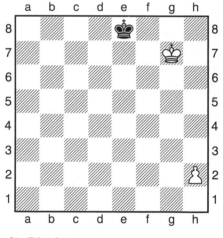

1) White/Black to move

Black to move draws with 1...♔f7 2 h4 ♔f8 3 h5 ♔f7 4 h6 ♔f8 5 ♔g6 ♔g8 6 h7+ ♔h8 7 ♔h6 stalemate. If White is to move, he wins with 1 ♔g7 *(2)*.

2) Black to move

White's king has reached a key square and the pawn queens sooner or later: 1...♔e7 2 h4 ♔e6 3 h5 ♔f5 4 h6 ♔g5 5 h7 and White wins.

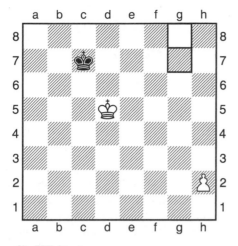

3) White to move

Here the kings fight for the key squares: 1 ♔e6 (the king advances first as 1 h4? allows Black to draw by 1...♚d7, since his king will reach the h8-corner in time) 1...♚d8 (4).

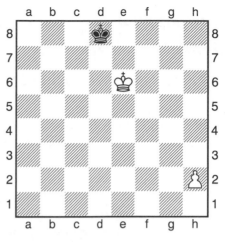

4) White to move

The white king now blocks his black counterpart's access to e8 and e7: 2 ♔f7 ♚d7 3 h4 ♚d6 4 h5 ♚e5 5 h6 and White wins.

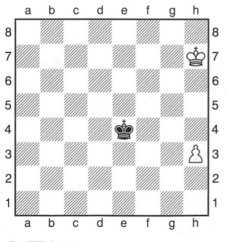

5) White to move

A typical mistake is to advance the pawn too early: 1 h4? (in order to win, the king must first give a bodycheck with 1 ♔g6!) 1...♚f5 2 h5 ♚f6 (6).

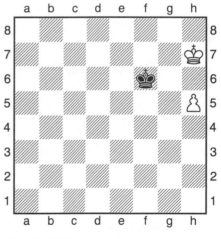

6) White to move

White surprisingly can't win despite the fact that he can reach a key square: it is a draw after 3 h6 ♚f7, 3 ♔h6 ♚f7 or 3 ♔g8 ♚g5. So this is a non-trivial exception.

<table>
<tr>
<td>

ENDGAME LESSON 10

</td>
<td>

King and Pawn Each: Blocked Pawns

</td>
</tr>
</table>

Not all critical squares are key squares

Now we consider endings with king and pawn vs king and pawn where the pawns are blocking each other. That means it is purely a battle between the kings, at least until one of the pawns is captured.

We define a *critical* square as one that, if reached by the attacking king, it can force the capture of the enemy pawn. Those squares are as follows: the three squares nearest the pawn on its same rank, and the square behind the last of those three. So for a black pawn on g6, the critical squares are f6, e6, d6 and d7. If White's king can reach them then he will win the g6-pawn. As g6 is a key square for a white pawn on g5, White wins, so in this case the critical squares are key squares.

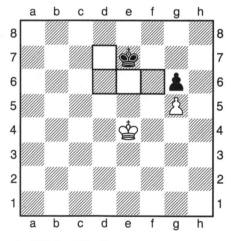

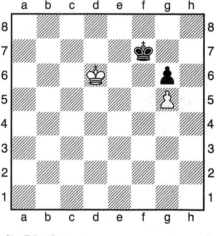

1) White/Black to move

If Black is to play, then he should choose 1...♔e6 – see diagram 4. If White is to move, he can win by taking the opposition: 1 ♔e5 ♔f7 2 ♔d6 *(2)*.

2) Black to move

The king has reached a key square. 2...♔f8 3 ♔e6 ♔g7 4 ♔e7 ♔g8 5 ♔f6 ♔h7 6 ♔f7 ♔h8 7 ♔xg6 ♔g8 *(3)*.

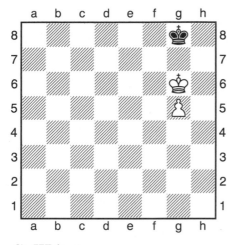

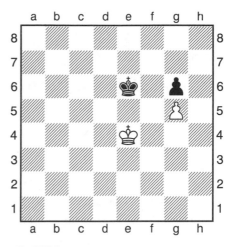

3) White to move

An important moment. After 8 ♔f6?! ♚h7 White must repeat with 9 ♔f7 ♚h8 10 ♔g6 as 9 g6+? ♚h8 10 ♔f7 is stalemate. Instead he wins by 8 ♔h6! ♚h8 9 g6 ♚g8 10 g7 ♚f7 11 ♚h7.

4) White to move

Now the white pawn on g5 is lost, but White can nevertheless draw by defending the resulting key squares: 2 ♔f4 ♚d5 *(5)*.

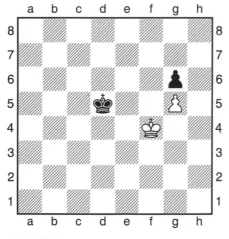

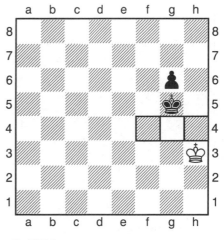

5) White to move

The black king has reached a critical square. 3 ♔f3 ♚e5 4 ♔g4 ♚e4 5 ♔g3 ♚f5 6 ♔h4 ♚f4 7 ♔h3 ♚xg5 *(6)*.

6) White to move

Black has won the white pawn, but he cannot win the game. After 8 ♔g3! White's king defends the key squares (f4, g4 and h4) by taking the opposition.

11 King and Pawn Each: Pawn Races

Calculate and run but do not just count the moves

Now we look at king and pawn vs king and pawn but with the pawns on different files. They can either be on adjacent files (so no passed pawns) or further apart (i.e. both passed pawns).

These two situations are totally different. Pawns on adjacent files have a very large drawish tendency. The defender can usually hold either by protecting his own pawn or by counterattacking the enemy pawn.

Races between passed pawns are different of course. Just counting the moves needed to promote is not a good idea as the pawn might promote with check or the new-born queen might be lost directly. We see this clearly in diagram 3, where both sides would queen at the same time if they simply advanced their pawns, but White wins thanks to a neat trick.

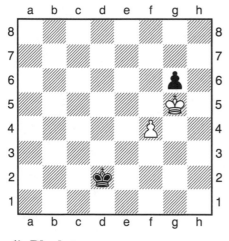

1) Black to move

The draw is clear after 1...♚e3! and now 2 ♔xg6 ♚xf4 or 2 ♔g4 ♚e4 3 ♔g5 ♚f3.

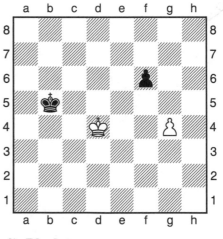

2) Black to move

Here Black's king is in time to defend the pawn: 1...♚c6 2 ♔e4 ♚d6 3 ♔f5 ♚e7 4 ♔g6 ♚e6 and Black draws.

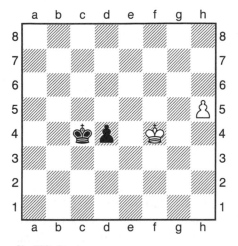

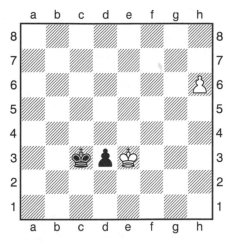

3) White to move

It looks like the race will end in a draw, but White has 1 h6! d3 2 ♔e3! (forcing Black's king onto an unfortunate square; not 2 ♔f3? ♔b3!, drawing) 2...♔c3 *(4)*.

4) White to move

Now White will queen with check and Black not at all: 3 h7 d2 4 h8♕+ ♔c2 5 ♕h2 ♔c1 6 ♕xd2+, winning.

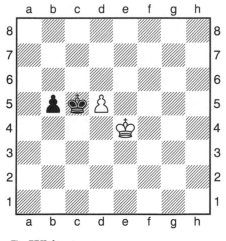

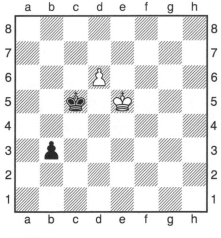

5) White to move

White wins Black's new-born queen in the critical variation: 1 ♔e5 b4 (1...♔b6 2 d6 ♔b7 3 ♔e6 b4 4 d7 ♔c7 5 ♔e7 and White wins) 2 d6 b3 *(6)*.

6) White to move

Now both sides will queen, which usually leads to a draw. But here matters are different: 3 d7 b2 4 d8♕ b1♕ 5 ♕c7+ ♔b4 6 ♕b6+, winning.

King Geometry

On the chessboard the king is as quick on a diagonal as on a straight line

This is in sharp contrast to standard geometry, where the diagonal is longer. Due to this very important observation the king can often pursue two aims simultaneously without any cost in time – sometimes called 'hunting two hares'.

I have included three famous examples of this startling phenomenon. The first is a really amazing study by Richard Réti, which is one of the most famous chess positions of all time. At first sight it looks completely unbelievable to the human eye that White's king can catch Black's h-pawn.

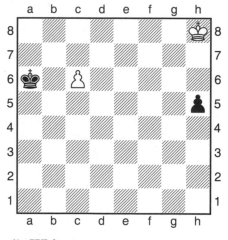

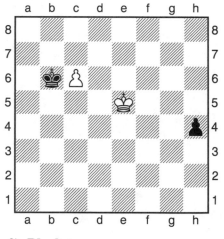

1) White to move

White's king must find a way to help the c-pawn and stop the h-pawn. To do so, it moves diagonally: 1 ♔g7 h4 2 ♔f6 ♔b6 (2...h3 3 ♔e7 is a draw) 3 ♔e5 *(2)*.

2) Black to move

Now White has two threats (♔d6 and ♔f4) and Black can parry only one of them. Both 3...♔xc6 4 ♔f4 and 3...h3 4 ♔d6 h2 5 c7 h1♕ 6 c8♕ are drawn.

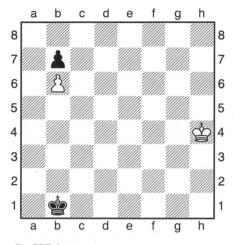

3) White to move

This is the end of a study by Grigoriev. White's king has 141 routes to b4 if Black's king is ignored, but only one draws: 1 ♔g3 ♔c2 2 ♔f2 ♔d3 *(4)*.

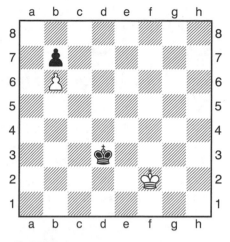

4) White to move

Now 3 ♔e1 avoids being shouldered away: 3...♔c4 4 ♔d2 ♔b5 5 ♔c3 ♔xb6 6 ♔b4, with a draw.

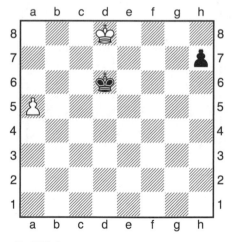

5) White to move

This is a study by de Feijter: 1 ♔c8 (1 a6? loses to 1...♔c6 2 ♔c8 ♔b6 3 ♔d7 h5) 1...♔c6 2 ♔b8 ♔b5 *(6)*.

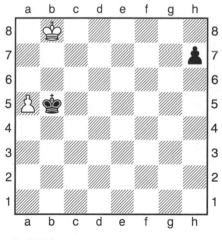

6) White to move

3 ♔b7! and White's king will reach the square of the passed pawn: 3...♔xa5 4 ♔c6 h5 5 ♔d5 h4 6 ♔e4, with a draw.

Protected Passed Pawn

Are all the key squares in the square of the passed pawn?

Here we are looking at king and two pawns vs king and one pawn, where the extra pawn is both passed and protected by its colleague. Usually the attacker wins, but there are two important exceptions. If the protected passed pawn is too far advanced and near the edge of the board, then stalemate can rescue the defender. Or if all the key squares are inside the square of the protected passed pawn and the defending king can win the battle for the opposition.

A general definition of the opposition is that all four corners of the rectangle surrounding the kings should have the same colour. This generalizes the simple opposition that we saw in Lesson 8. Diagrams 4 and 5 show forms of the opposition.

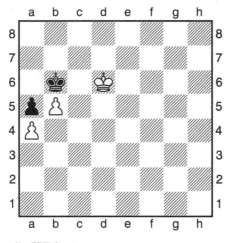

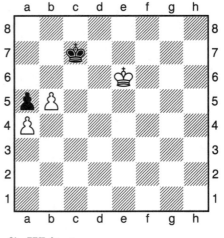

1) White to move

The attacker usually wins; White's king could even be very far away and he would still win. After 1 ♔e6 Black cannot keep the opposition. 1...♔c7 *(2)*.

2) White to move

2 ♔e7 ♔c8 3 ♔d6 ♔b7 4 ♔d7 and White wins after 4...♔b6 5 ♔c8 ♔a7 6 ♔c7 or 4...♔b8 5 ♔c6 ♔a7 6 ♔c7 ♔a8 7 ♔b6.

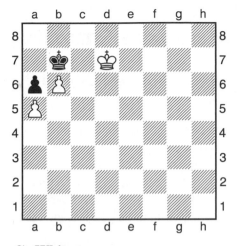

3) White to move

This is an important exception as the edge is too close: 1 ♔d6 ♚c8 2 ♔c6 ♚b8 3 b7 ♚a7 4 ♔c7 stalemate.

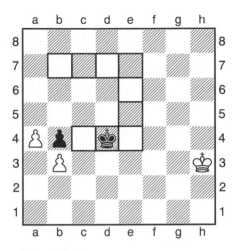

4) Black to move

This is also drawn as all the key squares are inside the square of the passed a-pawn: 1...♚d5! *(5)*.

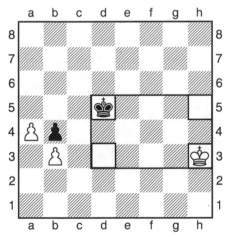

5) White to move

Black has the virtual opposition. The corners (d5, d3, h3 and h5) are all light. 2 ♔g3 ♚e5 is diagonal opposition as the corners of the rectangle around the kings – g3, g5, e5 and e3 – are all dark. 3 ♔g4 ♚e4 4 ♔h5 ♚d5 with a draw.

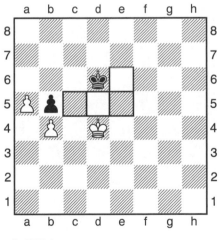

6) White to move

This time the key squares on the e-file are not in the square of the passed a-pawn: 1 ♔e4 ♚c6 2 ♔e5 and White wins.

ENDGAME LESSON 14 Triangulation and More Opposition

The triangle can work wonders as three is not an even number

Here we look at further positions with king and two pawns vs king and one pawn. If the extra pawn is a passed pawn but not a *protected* passed pawn, the attacker also usually wins easily. The passed pawn deflects the defending king and the attacking king can win the defender's pawn and then win with the remaining pawn. But there are difficult cases, especially when blocked rook's pawns are involved. With an additional bishop's pawn, the win using *triangulation* is worth knowing. For the case that the passed pawn is further away, see Lesson 15.

The final four diagrams show how the kings fight for vital squares when there are no passed pawns.

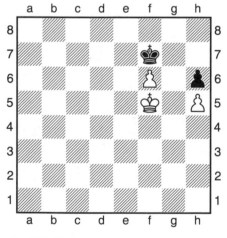

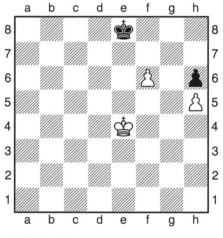

1) White to move

White wins by transferring the move to Black: 1 ♔e5 ♔f8 (Black can't mirror the manoeuvre because e7 is covered by the f6-pawn) 2 ♔f4 ♔e8 3 ♔e4 (2). This triangle manoeuvre puts Black in a fatal zugzwang.

2) Black to move

White wins since ...♔g8 is illegal, and 3...♔f7 loses directly to 4 ♔f5 ♔f8 5 ♔g6. That leaves 3...♔f8 4 ♔e5 ♔e8 5 ♔e6 ♔f8 6 f7 ♔g7 7 ♔e7 ♔h7 8 ♔f6, when White wins.

38

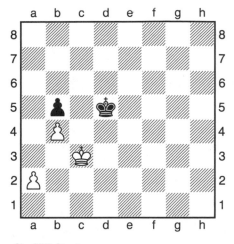

3) White to move

The triangle also helps here: 1 ♔b3 ♔c6 2 ♔b2 ♔d6 3 ♔c2 (the triangle is completed) 3...♔d5 4 ♔c3 ♔c6 5 ♔d4 ♔d6 6 a3 (a vital 'tempo move' to put Black in zugzwang) 6...♔c6 7 ♔e5 and White wins.

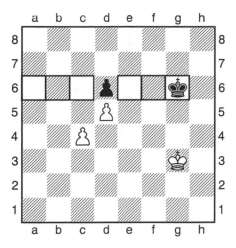

4) Black to move

In general the attacker can't use triangulation in such situations (Black can also 'triangulate' in reply) and opposition is the main fighting method for the key squares: 1...♔g7! *(5)* (for 1...♔g5?, see diagram 6).

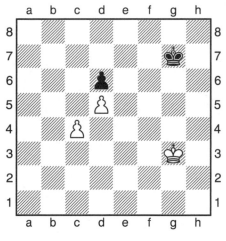

5) White to move

Black has taken the distant opposition, and draws: 2 ♔f3 ♔f7! 3 ♔f4 ♔f6 4 ♔e3 ♔e7 5 ♔d4 ♔d7 6 ♔c3 ♔c7 7 ♔b4 ♔b6.

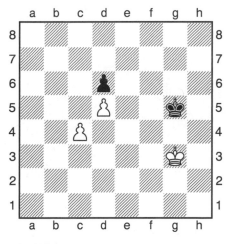

6) White to move

White wins with 2 ♔f3 ♔f5 3 ♔e3 ♔e5 4 ♔d3 ♔f6 (Black can't get to the queenside in time) 5 ♔c3 ♔e7 6 ♔b4 ♔d7 7 ♔b5 ♔c7 8 ♔a6.

ENDGAME LESSON 15

Bähr's Rule

Draw those diagonals to draw the conclusion

Now we consider a pair of blocked pawns with an extra pawn for the attacker several files away. If the attacking king can support the passed pawn, he usually wins (see also Lesson 14). But there is an important exception, if the blocked pawns are on a rook's file. Let's assume they are on the a-file. If the extra pawn is on the d-, e-, f-, g- or h-file then Bähr's Rule can help us assess the position.

This rule has two parts. Both kings must be in position near the pawn as in the first diagram below. If the attacker's rook's pawn has crossed the middle of the board, the attacker wins. If not then draw a diagonal from the *defender's* pawn towards the eighth rank and from the point of intersection with the c-file back towards the first rank. (This sounds complex but the diagrams should make it clearer.) If the attacking passed pawn has *not* crossed this diagonal, then the attacker wins.

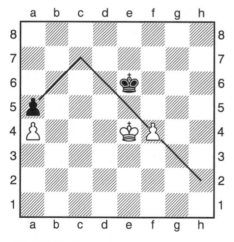

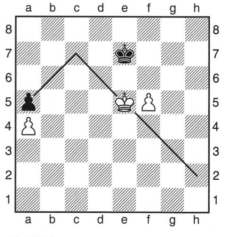

1) White to move

For the correct 1 ♔d4!, see diagram 3. Instead, 1 f5+? is a typical mistake: 1...♔f6 2 ♔f4 ♔f7 3 ♔e5 ♔e7 *(2)*.

2) White to move

This is drawn, since the f-pawn has crossed the c7-h2 diagonal: 4 ♔d5 ♔f6 5 ♔c5 ♔xf5 6 ♔b5 ♔e6 7 ♔xa5 ♔d7 8 ♔b6 ♔c8 with a draw (see Lesson 9).

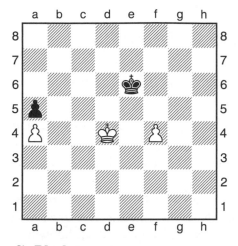

3) Black to move

White wins the race of the kings, as Bähr's Rule predicts: 1...♔f5 2 ♔c5 ♔xf4 3 ♔b5 ♔e5 4 ♔xa5 ♔d6 5 ♔b6 ♔d7 6 ♔b7, winning.

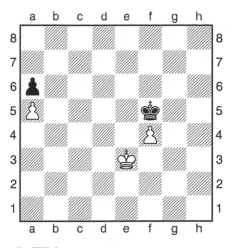

4) White to move

The a5-pawn has crossed the middle of the board, so White wins as a rule. But the direct 1 ♔d4? runs into 1...♔xf4 2 ♔c5 ♔e5 3 ♔b6 ♔d6 4 ♔xa6 ♔c7, drawing. The king must first gain space: 1 ♔f3! ♔f6 2 ♔e4 ♔e6 (5).

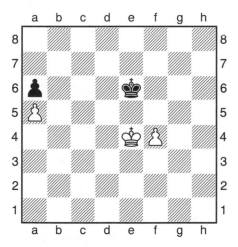

5) White to move

Now White can head for the a-pawn: 3 ♔d4 ♔f5 4 ♔c5 ♔xf4 5 ♔b6 ♔e5 6 ♔xa6 ♔d6 7 ♔b7, winning.

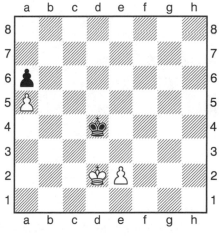

6) White to move

There are exceptions if the passed pawn is far behind. Here a counterattack saves Black: 1 e3+ ♔c4 2 ♔e2 ♔b4 3 e4 ♔xa5 4 e5 ♔b6, with a draw.

41

Pawns on One Wing

Invasions, battering-rams and stalemate cages

Now we consider pawn endings where both players have a few pawns, starting with the case where they are all on one side of the board. As usual the attacking king should advance first to gain as much space as possible. Then it will be clearer what to do with the pawns.

The drawing margin in this type of ending is often not very large. A slight advantage in space can be decisive, as in the first diagram, where a battering-ram undermines Black's pawn-structure. But there are also defensive techniques worth knowing of course, like the stalemate cage from diagram 3.

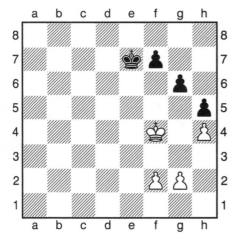

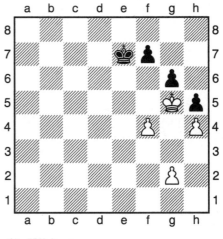

1) White to move

First White's king invades: 1 ♔g5 ♔e6 (for 1...♔f8 see diagram 3) 2 f4 (the battering-ram moves into position) 2...♔e7 *(2)*.

2) White to move

Now White's battering-ram undermines Black's pawn-structure: 3 f5 gxf5 4 ♔xf5 ♔f8 5 ♔g5 ♔g7 6 ♔xh5 ♔f6 7 ♔g4 ♔g6 8 ♔f4 ♔h5 9 g3 and White wins.

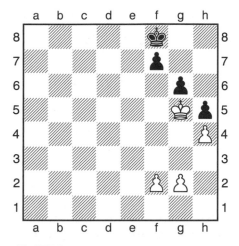

3) White to move

The procedure here is similar: 2 ♔f6 (the king advances first) 2...♔g8 3 f4 (only now is the battering-ram moved into position) 3...♔f8 *(4)*.

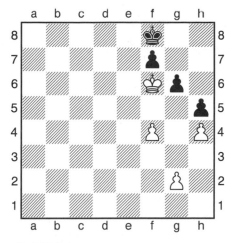

4) White to move

4 f5 shatters the foundations of Black's pawn-chain: 4...gxf5 5 ♔xf5 ♔g7 6 ♔g5 ♔h7 7 ♔xh5 f6 *(5)*.

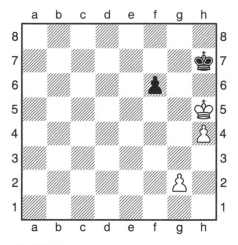

5) White to move

Now comes the final phase: 8 ♔g4 ♔g6 9 ♔f4 ♔h5 10 g3 ♔g6 11 g4 ♔g7 12 ♔f5 ♔f7 13 h5 ♔g7 14 ♔e6 and White wins.

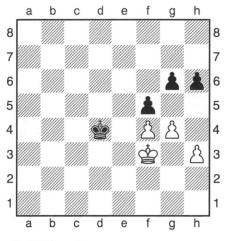

6) White to move

White must build a stalemate cage to survive: 1 g5 h5 (1...hxg5 2 fxg5 ♔e5 3 h4 f4 4 h5 gxh5 5 g6 is also drawn) 2 ♔g3 ♔e3 3 ♔h4 ♔xf4 stalemate.

The Outside Passed Pawn

Often the outsider weighs heavier than an active king

Now we move on to situations where there are pawns on both sides of the board. We start with positions where both players have a few pawns on one side of the board, but one player also has a passed pawn far away on the other wing. This is called an *outside* passed pawn. It is a powerful asset in many types of endgame, but especially so in a pawn ending as there is only the defending king left to deal with it. Thus the king is deflected from the other wing, which is then defenceless against an invasion by the attacking king. But an outside passed pawn does not win automatically, as diagram 3 shows.

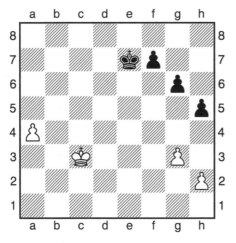

1) White to move

This is from the famous game Fischer-Larsen, Candidates (5), Denver 1971: 41 ♔d4 ♚d6 42 a5 (the outside passed a-pawn deflects Black's king) 42...f6 (2).

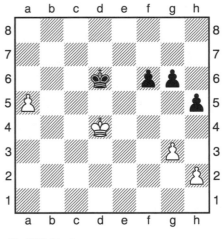

2) White to move

43 a6 ♚c6 44 a7 ♚b7 45 ♔d5 h4 46 ♔e6 and Black resigned; e.g., 46...hxg3 47 hxg3 f5 48 ♔f6 ♚xa7 49 ♔xg6.

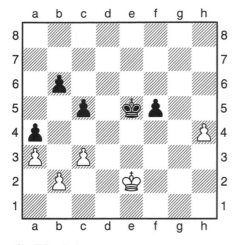

3) Black to move

This position, from the game Englisch-Steinitz, London 1883, is an exception, as Black's active king proves a more important factor: 39...♚f4 40 c4 ♚g4 41 ♚e3 *(4)*.

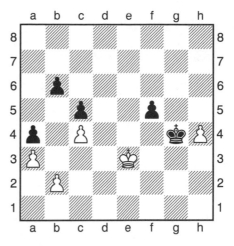

4) Black to move

41...f4+! (the greedy 41...♚xh4? runs into 42 ♚f4!, drawing) 42 ♚e4 f3 43 ♚e3 ♚g3 and White resigned due to 44 h5 f2 45 ♚e2 ♚g2.

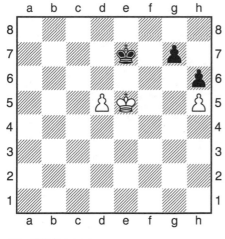

5) White to move

Against a crippled majority (Black's two pawns are held back by one white pawn), the outside passed pawn can often be used as follows: 1 d6+ ♚d7 2 ♚d5 ♚d8 3 ♚e6 ♚e8 4 d7+ ♚d8 5 ♚d6 *(6)*.

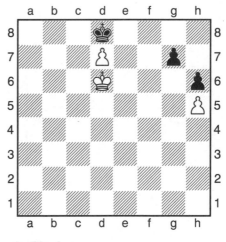

6) Black to move

Now Black must throw himself on his own sword: 5...g5 6 hxg6 (this *en passant* capture is the reason why the majority can't be mobilized) 6...h5 7 g7 h4 8 g8♛#.

ENDGAME LESSON 18

Mobilizing a Pawn-Majority

Candidate first

Now we take a look at endings where there are pawns on both wings, but no passed pawns – yet. When one player has more pawns than his opponent on one side of the board, he is said to have a *majority*. Unless this majority is weakened in some way, it has the potential to produce a passed pawn. The most likely pawn to become passed is the one that has no enemy pawn on the same file – this pawn is called a *candidate*. Usually a majority is mobilized by moving the candidate first to avoid any backward pawns. Then the other pawns advance carefully to create a passed pawn. Of course, this should only be done when the time is right. Often the king should advance first, while sometimes the majority should make a breakthrough in another way (see diagram 5).

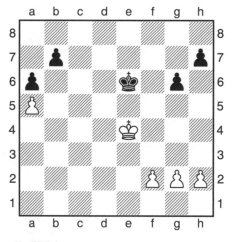

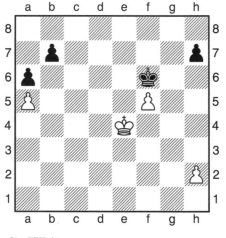

1) White to move

The f-pawn is the candidate: 1 f4! ♔d6 (for 1...h5, see diagram 3) 2 g4 ♔e6 (or 2...♔c6 3 f5 and White wins) 3 f5+ gxf5+ 4 gxf5+ ♔f6 *(2)*.

2) White to move

White wins with the technique seen in diagram 5 of Lesson 17: 5 ♔f4 ♔f7 6 ♔e5 ♔e7 7 f6+ ♔f7 8 ♔f5 ♔f8 9 ♔e6 ♔e8 10 f7+ ♔f8 11 ♔f6 h5 12 h4.

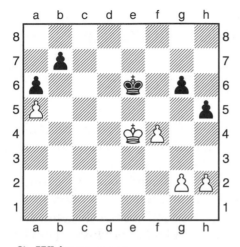

3) White to move

Now White has to be careful: 2 g3! (2 h3? allows 2...h4, drawing) 2...♚d6 3 h3 ♚c6 4 g4 hxg4 5 hxg4 b5 6 axb6 ♚xb6 *(4)*.

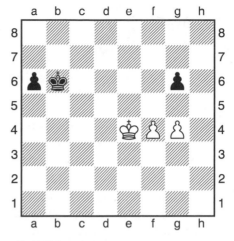

4) White to move

This is an exception to the 'candidate first' rule: 7 g5!! (7 f5? allows Black to draw by 7...gxf5+ 8 gxf5 ♚c7) 7...a5 *(5)* (for 7...♚c7 see diagram 6).

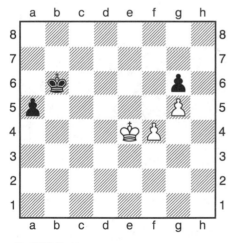

5) White to move

Now comes the breakthrough by the majority: 8 f5 gxf5+ (8...a4 loses to 9 f6) 9 ♚d3 a4 10 g6 a3 11 ♚c2 a2 12 ♚b2 f4 13 g7 f3 14 g8♛ and White wins.

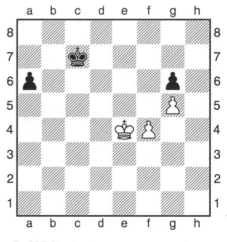

6) White to move

White is quicker: 8 f5 gxf5+ 9 ♚xf5 ♚d7 10 ♚f6 ♚e8 11 ♚g7 a5 12 g6 a4 13 ♚h7 a3 14 g7 a2 15 g8♛+, winning.

Pawn Breakthrough

Shocking, surprising... and often decisive

We shall finish our investigation of pawn endings with a look at a violent tactical idea that adds an extra dimension to the play: the breakthrough. They are easily overlooked, and can help both attacker and defender, so you need to be on the lookout for them. As a passed pawn is very valuable, it is often worth considering creating one by sacrificing other pawns. In the previous lesson we saw an example in diagram 5. But sometimes a majority is not even needed and an equal number of pawns suffices (see diagrams 1 and 2). Especially with far-advanced pawns (see diagram 1) or broken pawn-structures (see diagram 2), care is called for. In very special cases, even a minority can make a breakthrough (see diagram 6).

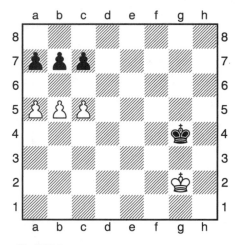

1) White to move

This old study by Cozio is famous: 1 b6!! cxb6 (1...axb6 2 c6 bxc6 3 a6 is similar) 2 a6 bxa6 3 c6 and White wins.

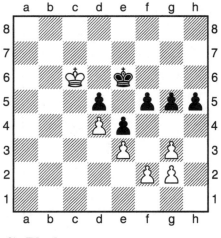

2) Black to move

Broken structures can invite breakthroughs. This is Svacina-H.Müller, Vienna 1941. After 1...g4 2 ♔c5 f4!! *(3)* White cannot stop the wave of pawns.

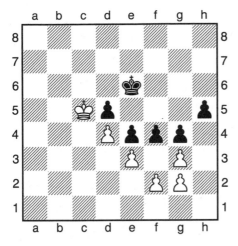

3) White to move

3 exf4 (3 gxf4 h4 and 3 ♔b4 f3 4 gxf3
exf3 5 ♔c3 h4 6 gxh4 g3 7 fxg3 f2 are also
winning for Black) 3...h4 4 gxh4 g3 5 fxg3
e3 and Black wins.

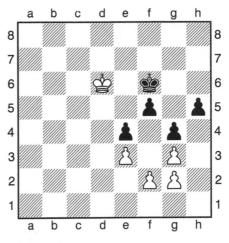

4) Black to move

Pomar-Cuadras, Olot 1974 is similar:
42...f4!! 43 ♔d5 (Black wins after 43 gxf4
h4 or 43 exf4 h4 44 gxh4 g3 45 fxg3 e3)
43...h4 44 ♔xe4 *(5)*.

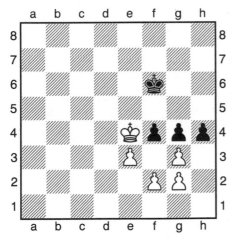

5) Black to move

The game ended 44...f3! 45 gxf3 h3 46
fxg4 h2 47 f3 h1♕ 48 ♔f4 ♕h6+ 49 ♔e4
♕g5 50 ♔d4 ♕e5+ 0-1.

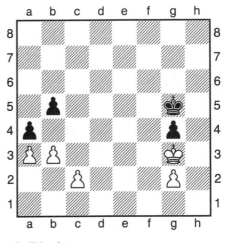

6) Black to move

White last move, 1 b3??, was a blunder
due to 1...b4!, when Black's minority
breaks through. He wins after 2 axb4 a3 or
2 bxa4 bxa3.

Knight against Pawns

Knight geometry and the magical square

We now consider endings with just knights and pawns. The knight's unusual way of moving gives it some unique features. It changes the colour of the square on which it stands with every move and so it can't lose a tempo. An awkwardly-placed knight can be dominated by a well-placed king. On the other hand, the knight's forking ability can enable it to perform remarkable feats, such as creating barriers against the enemy king on an open board.

Usually a knight can stop a single pawn on its own, provided it can control one square in front of the pawn. But there is one important exception. A rook's pawn on its seventh rank cannot be stopped by the knight alone; the defending king must lend a helping hand. Surprisingly, against a king trapped in front of a far-advanced rook's pawn, the knight can even win without friendly pawns.

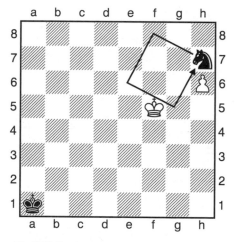

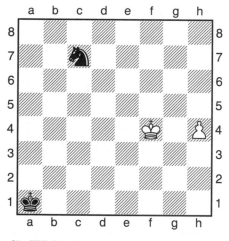

1) White to move

The knight can stop the pawn on its own: 1 ♔g6 ♘f8+ 2 ♔g7 ♘e6+ 3 ♔f7 ♘g5+ 4 ♔g6 ♘e6 5 h7 ♘f8+, with a draw.

2) White to move

The knight must be dominated first: with 1 ♔e5! *(3)* the king moves into the 'knight check shadow'. The knight needs three moves to give check.

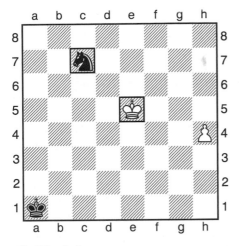

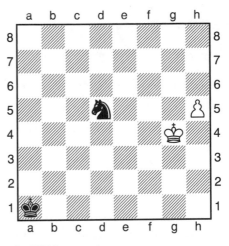

3) Black to move

The knight can't stop the pawn: 1...♞e8 2 h5 ♞g7 3 h6 (remember: a knight on g7 loses against a pawn on h6) 3...♞e8 4 h7 and White wins.

4) White to move

Again White must dominate the knight first: 1 ♔g5 (5). This domination might be called the 'Karpov Distance' since he is a great master at dominating the enemy knights.

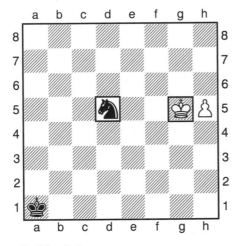

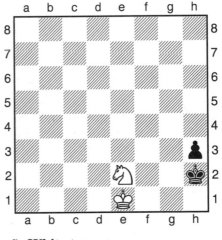

5) Black to move

1...♞c7 (1...♞e7 loses to 2 h6) 2 ♔f5 ♞d5 3 h6 ♞e7+ 4 ♔g5 (the king moves into the 'knight check shadow') 4...♞g8 5 h7 and White wins.

6) White to move

Here we see an idea known as Stamma's Mate, in which the black king is fatally trapped in front of its own pawn: 1 ♔f1! ♔h1 2 ♔f2 ♔h2 3 ♞d4 ♔h1 4 ♞f5 ♔h2 5 ♞e3 ♔h1 6 ♞f1 h2 7 ♞g3#.

Extra Knight

Sources of tempi, wrong feet and other oddities

Now we consider positions where the player with the knight also has some pawns and is the side trying to win. The knight's superiority over pawns is not as large as the bishop, since the knight is a short-range piece and can prove clumsy. You should be aware of the following guidelines:

1) The knight should protect a passed pawn from behind (see diagram 1).

2) The knight can't lose a tempo; this is usually the king's job (see diagrams 2 and 3).

3) The knight changes the colour of the square on which it stands with every move. So it has a 'parity' and can be 'on the wrong foot'.

4) The king should support a friendly passed pawn, while the knight blockades the enemy pawns (see diagram 5).

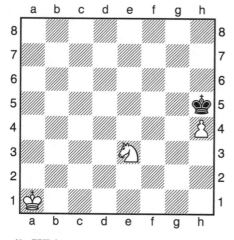

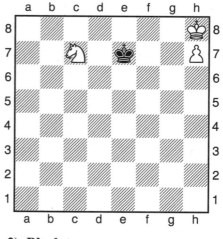

1) White to move

The knight must protect the passed pawn from behind: 1 ♘g2! (1 ♘f5? is met by 1...♚g4, drawing) 1...♚g4 2 ♚b2 ♚g3 3 h5 and White wins.

2) Black to move

Amazingly this is drawn after 1...♚f8 (1...♚f7? loses to 2 ♘e6) 2 ♘e6+ ♚f7 as the knight is on the wrong foot and unable to lose a tempo.

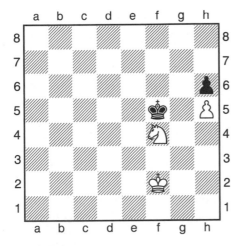

3) White to move

The king must move to the right square: 1 ♔g3? (only 1 ♔f3! ♔g5 2 ♔g3 ♔f5 3 ♘h3 wins) 1...♔g5 2 ♔f3 ♔h4 (4).

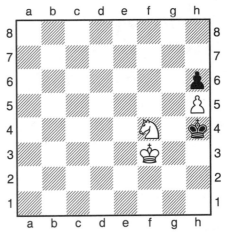

4) White to move

The knight is fixed in place and White can't reorganize his pieces successfully: 3 ♔e4 ♔g4 4 ♔e5 ♔g5 5 ♔e6 ♔xf4 6 ♔f6 ♔e4 7 ♔g6 ♔e5 8 ♔xh6 ♔f6 with a draw.

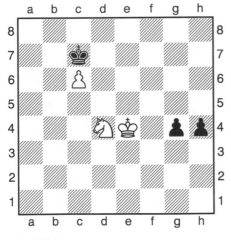

5) White to move

The king should support White's passed pawn: 1 ♔d5! h3 (1...g3 2 ♘e2 g2 3 ♘g1 is a similar win for White) 2 ♘f5 h2 3 ♘g3 ♔c8 (6).

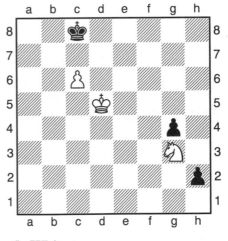

6) White to move

Now White wins as the knight acts as a source of tempi: 4 ♔d6 ♔d8 5 c7+ ♔c8 6 ♘h1 ♔b7 7 ♔d7.

Knight Endgames

Botvinnik's Law and Fine's Fine Rule

According to the principle stated by former world champion Mikhail Botvinnik, knight endings are like pawn endings. While this shouldn't be taken too literally, they have more similarities to pawn endings than do endings with other pieces. In knight endings, an outside passed pawn is a very strong asset, and zugzwang plays a major role (like in pawn endings) as the knight can't lose a tempo (see Lesson 21). But there are differences of course. There are tactical knight tricks and sacrifices that you will obviously not see in a pawn ending.

Reuben Fine's rule is also unique to knight endings: with knight and pawn vs knight, a pawn on its seventh rank wins if it is supported by its king, unless the defender can force an immediate draw.

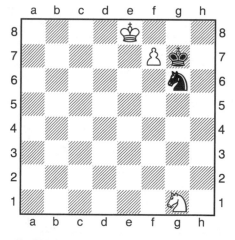

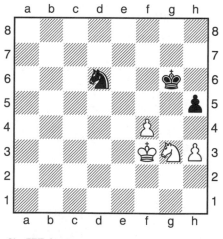

1) White to move

White's king supports the passed pawn, so Fine's Rule predicts a win, which is indeed the case: 1 ♘f3 ♚f6 2 ♘h4 ♘xh4 3 f8♕+.

2) White to move

In Postny-Apicella, Metz 2009, White used zugzwang: 83 h4 ♘b7 (83...♘f5 84 ♘xf5 ♚xf5 85 ♚e3 ♚g4 86 ♚e4 ♚xh4 87 ♚f3 is winning for White) 84 f5+ ♚h6 *(3)*.

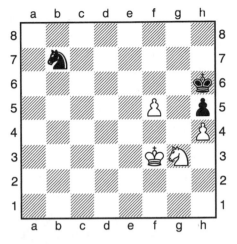

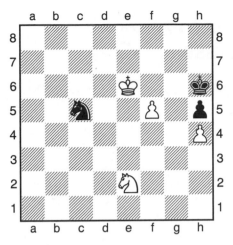

3) White to move

Now White's king advances: 85 ♔e4 ♞c5+ 86 ♔d4 ♞b3+ 87 ♔d5 ♞c1 88 ♔e6 ♞d3 89 ♞e2 ♞c5+ *(4)*.

4) White to move

90 ♔e7 ♞d3 91 f6 ♞e5 92 ♞f4 ♞c6+ 93 ♔e8 1-0. The extra pawn was converted into victory despite the reduced number of pawns.

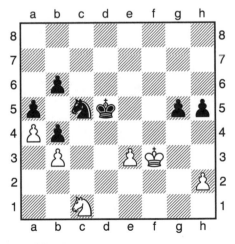

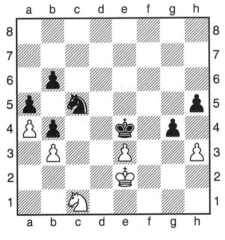

5) Black to move

In S.Ivanov-Emelin, St Petersburg Ch 2009, Black exploited the outside majority: 41...♔e5 42 h3 ♔d5 43 ♔f2 ♔e4 44 ♔e2 g4 *(6)*.

6) White to move

White resigned as he loses after 45 hxg4 hxg4 46 ♔f2 (or 46 ♔d2 ♔f3) 46...♞d3+ 47 ♞xd3 ♔xd3 48 ♔g3 ♔xe3 49 ♔xg4 ♔d4.

ENDGAME LESSON 23

Bishop against Pawns

The principle of one diagonal

The bishop usually has better chances than the knight in the fight against pawns due to its long-range capabilities. If all the key points the bishop must cover lie on one and the same diagonal, the bishop is very strong and cannot fall into zugzwang as long as the diagonal is long enough. However, if the bishop has work to do on two different diagonals, then it might become overloaded, and the king must assist in the fight against the enemy pawns.

A typical method for the bishop is to take aim at enemy pawns, either to tie the opposing king to their defence or to force them to advance in such a way that they can be blockaded.

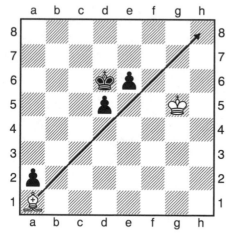

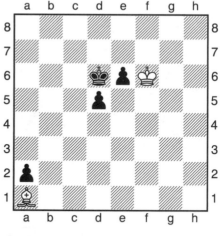

1) White to move

White halts the advance of all the black pawns on the long diagonal: 1 ♔f4 (for 1 ♔f6? see the next diagram) 1...♔c5 2 ♔e3 ♔c4 3 ♗e5 ♔b3 4 ♔d2, with a draw.

2) Black to move

Now Black can break through by 1...e5! 2 ♗xe5+ ♔c5 3 ♗a1 d4 4 ♔e5 d3 5 ♗c3 d2 6 ♗xd2 a1♕+, winning.

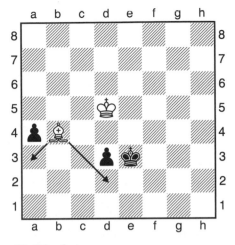

3) Black to move

Again the bishop has jobs on two different diagonals: 1...a3! (1...d2? allows a draw by 2 ♗xd2+ ♔xd2 3 ♔c4) 2 ♗xa3 d2 and Black wins.

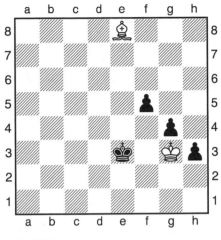

4) White to move

This position, from the game Tovmasin-Ilyin, Sochi 2012 is more difficult: 64 ♗d7! (the bishop takes aim at the pawns) 64...h2 (64...♔e4 is met by 65 ♗c8, when Black can't make progress) 65 ♔g2! *(5)* and a draw was agreed.

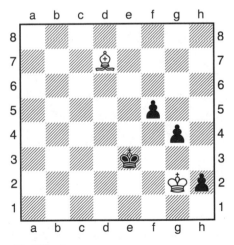

5) Black to move

One sample variation runs: 65...g3 66 ♗xf5 (for 66 ♔h1 see the next diagram) 66...h1♕+ 67 ♔xh1 ♔f2 68 ♗e4, with a draw.

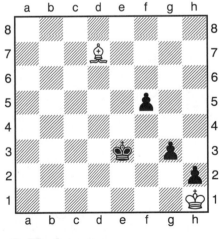

6) Black to move

Even this position is a draw as White can blockade the pawns: 66...♔f2 67 ♗c6 f4 68 ♗g2 f3 69 ♗xf3 ♔xf3 stalemate.

ENDGAME LESSON 24   Extra Bishop

The powerful endgame weapon zugzwang

The bishop is a very strong piece, so being a bishop up normally proves a decisive advantage, provided you have at least one pawn left. But a 'wrong' rook's pawn can create problems. The defender can draw as long as his king can reach the corner square in front of the rook's pawn. But aside from this special case, the bishop normally wins: first establish complete control and then zugzwang usually decides the game. The defender's best chance is to exchange off all the enemy pawns or else to construct a barrier. The reason zugzwang is especially powerful here is that the pawns usually run out of moves and then the defending king must give way step by step. But let's start with the 'wrong' rook's pawn, that is, the one whose promotion square can't be covered by the bishop.

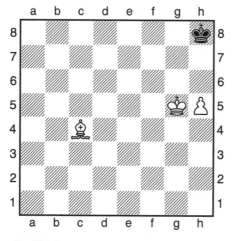

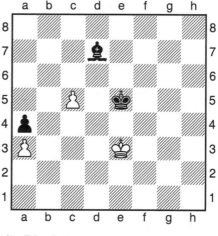

1) White to move

Surprisingly White can't win: 1 h6 ♚h7 2 ♗d3+ ♚g8 3 ♚g6 ♚h8 4 h7 stalemate. But if the defending king can't actually reach the corner, he may lose.

2) Black to move

In this position, from the game Ten Hertog-Kanarek, Albena 2011, White's king is too slow: 71...♗f5! 72 ♚d2 ♚d4 73 c6 ♚c4 74 c7 ♚b3 75 ♚c1 *(3)*.

58

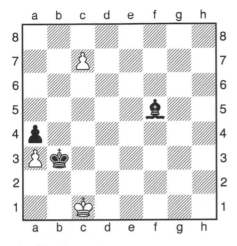

3) Black to move

White resigned due to 75...♔a2! (not 75...♔xa3?? when White can draw by 76 c8♕ ♗xc8 77 ♔b1) 76 ♔d2 ♔xa3 77 ♔c3 ♔a2 78 ♔b4 a3.

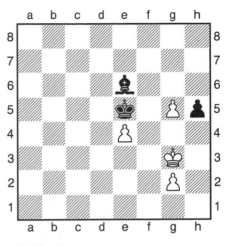

4) Black to move

This is from Siebrecht-S.Berger, German League 2010/11. Black has the 'right' rook's pawn and wins using zugzwang: 58...♗g4 (58...♔xe4? runs into 59 ♔h4 ♗f7 60 g4, drawing) 59 ♔h4 *(5)*.

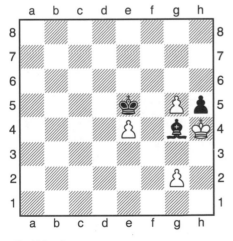

5) Black to move

59...♔e6! (Black wants to take on g5 with his king; the greedy 59...♔xe4? runs into 60 g6, drawing) 60 ♔g3 ♔f7 61 ♔f4 ♔g6 *(6)*.

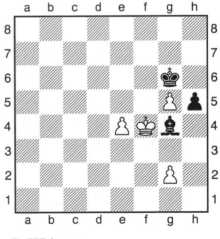

6) White to move

White is in zugzwang and will run out of pawn moves sooner or later: 62 ♔e5 (62 g3 ♗c8 63 e5 ♗e6 is winning for Black) 62...♔xg5 63 ♔d6 ♔f4 64 e5 ♔g3 65 e6 ♗xe6 0-1.

25 Same-Coloured Bishop Endings 1

Centurini's Rule

In the duel of bishop and pawn vs bishop, Centurini's Rule is most important, if the defending king can't get safely in front of the pawn. The configuration is seen in diagram 1. The defending king attacks the pawn and protects g6 so that White's bishop can't interfere. If both 'stopping diagonals' of the defending bishop are at least four squares long, then the defender draws according to Centurini's Rule; otherwise the attacker wins. There are two exceptions to this rule, both given by Centurini in 1856: w♔e8, ♗h6, ♙f7; b♚e6, ♝d6 and w♔g8, ♗e3, ♙h7; b♚g6, ♝e5 are drawn whoever moves first. Near the edge of the board, the attacker has problems winning; see diagram 4.

Note that here we are only talking about bishops that move on the same-coloured squares. With opposite-coloured bishops (see Lesson 27), these bishop and pawn vs bishop positions are drawn unless the pawn can promote immediately.

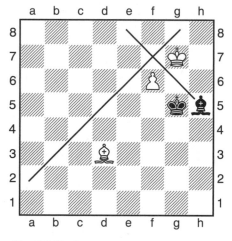

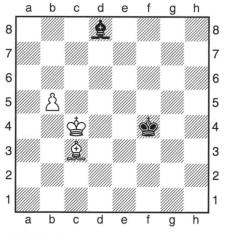

1) White to move

This is a draw as both stopping diagonals are longer than three squares: 1 ♗c4 ♗e8 2 ♗f7 ♗b5 3 ♗g6 ♗c4 and White can make no progress.

2) Black to move

In the game Taimanov-Fischer, Buenos Aires 1960, Fischer showed that he knew how to defend: 82...♚e4 83 ♗d4 ♝c7 84 ♔c5 *(3)*.

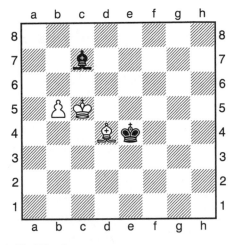

3) Black to move

The important point here is that the king needs to attack the pawn from behind: 84...♗d3! 85 ♔c6 ♔c4 86 ♗b6 ♗f4 87 ♗a7 ♗c7 ½-½.

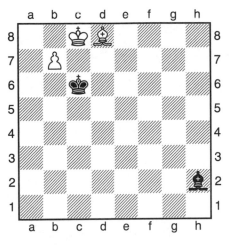

4) White to move

Centurini analysed this position in 1856. White can win, but it is far from simple: 1 ♗h4 ♔b6 2 ♗f2+ ♔a6 3 ♗c5! (zugzwang) 3...♗g3 4 ♗e7 ♔b6 5 ♗d8+ ♔c6 *(5)*.

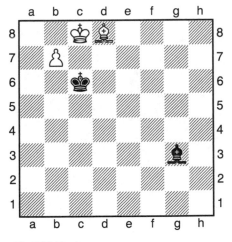

5) White to move

Now White can exploit the fact that Black's bishop has moved: 6 ♗h4! ♗h2 7 ♗f2 ♔b5 8 ♗a7 ♔c6 9 ♗b8 ♗g1 10 ♗e5 ♗a7 11 ♗d4 ♗xd4 12 b8♕ and White wins.

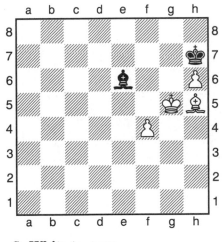

6) White to move

This is the game Fischer-Keres, Zurich 1959. White wins despite the wrong rook's pawn: 77 ♗g4 ♗c4 78 f5 ♗f7 79 ♗h5 ♗c4 80 ♔g6+ ♔g8 81 f6 1-0. White's king will move around to e7.

26 Same-Coloured Bishop Endings 2

Domination or Capablanca's Rule

With more pawns on the board, the attacker usually has a choice between placing his pawns on the same colour squares as the bishops to restrict the defending bishop or else to place them on the opposite colour to complement his own bishop and to fix the defending pawns on squares the bishop can attack – this strategy is also called Capablanca's Rule. Which strategy is better depends on the given position. Our first example shows an example of Capablanca's Rule and the second (starting from diagram 4) is an example where the restriction method is more appropriate.

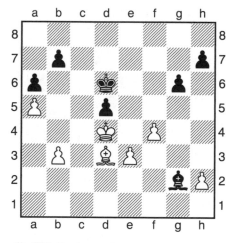

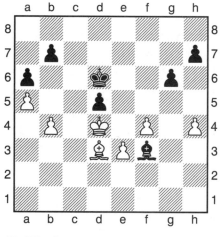

1) White to move

In this example, from the game Poluga-evsky-Mecking, Mar del Plata 1970, White followed Capablanca's Rule: 1 h4 ♗f3 2 b4 *(2)*.

2) Black to move

Now all the white pawns are on dark squares. 2...♗h1 3 ♗e2 ♗g2 4 ♗g4 ♗e4 5 ♗c8 ♔c7 6 ♗e6 ♔d6 7 ♗g8 h6 8 ♗f7 h5 9 ♗e8 ♗c2 10 ♗f7 ♗e4 *(3)*.

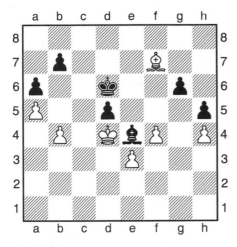

3) White to move

White won by 11 f5! ♗xf5 12 ♗xd5 ♗c8 13 e4 ♔e7 14 ♔e5 g5 15 hxg5 h4 16 g6 h3 17 g7 h2 18 g8♕ h1♕ 19 ♕f7+ ♔d8 20 ♕f8+ 1-0.

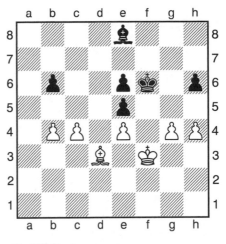

4) White to move

This position arose in Sulskis-Slekys, Lithuanian Ch, Vilnius 1994. White restricts Black's bishop: 1 b5! (1 c5? runs into 1...b5!, drawing) 1...♔e7 2 h5! (again restriction is called for) 2...♗d7 (5).

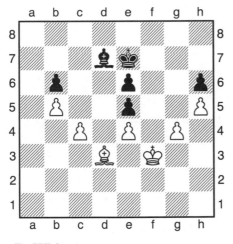

5) White to move

Now comes a breakthrough: 3 c5! bxc5 4 b6 ♗c8 5 g5! (and another one) 5...hxg5 6 h6 ♔f6 7 ♗c4 ♔g6 (6).

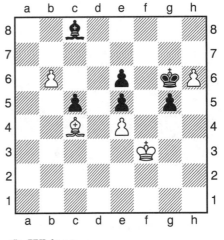

6) White to move

White won by 8 ♗xe6! ♗b7 (8...♗xe6 loses to 9 b7) 9 ♗d5 ♗c8 10 b7 ♗xb7 11 ♗xb7 c4 12 ♗c8 ♔xh6 13 ♗g4 1-0.

Opposite-Coloured Bishop Endings 1

They preach in different dioceses

Pure opposite-coloured bishop endings have a very strong drawish tendency as the bishops live in two different worlds. If the defender is securely dug in on squares the bishop can control, this is usually the end of the story and the game is drawn. Examples of such fortresses will be given in this lesson, and ways to break them in the following one. Usually the defending king blockades any passed pawns while the bishop protects the other wing, and all its jobs should be on one and the same diagonal. This diagonal needs to be long enough that the bishop can be neither put into zugzwang nor overloaded. Diagram 1 shows a typical fortress of this type. In another type of fortress, the defending bishop stops the pawns, while the king helps protect the diagonal and keeps the enemy king out. This will be seen in diagrams 2 and 6.

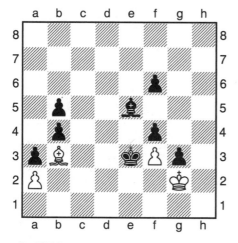

1) White to move

This is a typical fortress. White's bishop just waits on the b3-g8 diagonal for ever. 1 ♗f7 b3 2 ♗xb3 changes nothing.

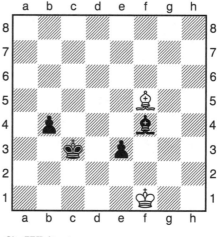

2) White to move

This example, from Berger-Kotlerman, Arkhangelsk 1948, shows a fortress of the second type: 1 ♔e2 b3 2 ♔d1 ♔b4 3 ♗h7 ♔a3 4 ♗g6 ♔b2 *(3)*.

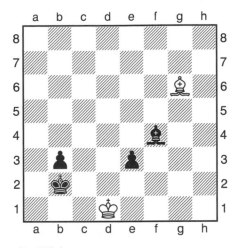

3) White to move

5 &f7! (the bishop takes aim at the pawn; not 5 &f5? &a1, when Black wins) 5...&a2 6 &e6 &a3 7 &f5! and the players agreed a draw in view of 7...b2 8 &b1 &b3 9 &e2.

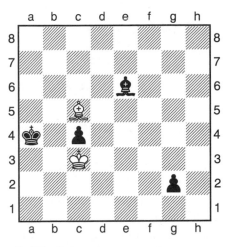

4) Black to move

If the pawns are four files apart they usually win, as in Oms Pallise-Salgado Lopez, Barcelona 2011: 83...&f7 84 &f2 &a3 85 &e3 &a2 86 &c2 &g6+ 87 &c3 &d3 88 &f2 &b1 89 &e3 &f1 *(5)* brings about the final zugzwang.

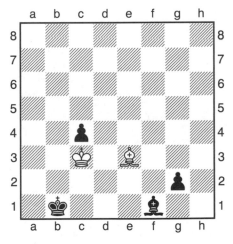

5) White to move

90 &g1 (90 &d2 &b2 91 &d4+ &b3 92 &c1 c3 wins for Black) 90...&c1 91 &f2 &d1 92 &d4 &d3 and White resigned in view of 93 &c3 &e2 and 93 &e3 c3.

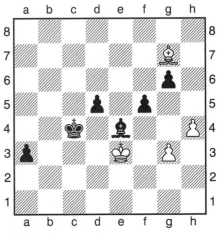

6) Black to move

White's bishop waits on the long diagonal and the king follows Black's: 1...&b3 2 &d2 &a2 3 &c1 &b3 4 &d2, holding the draw.

Opposite-Coloured Bishop Endings 2

The most amazing move ever?

Now we shall examine techniques to break a fortress. The most straightforward is that the attacking king simply invades. But this is often impossible and more violent means are required, such as pawn-breaks to create a passed pawn or to inject dynamism even at the cost of material. Pawn sacrifices are often justified, if the attacking bishop can control the resulting passed enemy pawns. The first diagram shows such a scenario. In diagram 4, even the attacking bishop is sacrificed to destroy a fortress based on the principle of one diagonal. Despite their logical motivation, ideas of this type are often very hard to foresee, due to their paradoxical nature and because they are unique to opposite-coloured bishop endings.

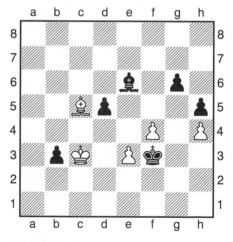

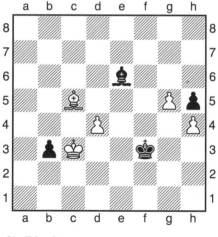

1) Black to move

This is Kotov-Botvinnik, USSR Ch, Moscow 1955. Black must act: 1...g5!! 2 fxg5 (2 ♔xb3 gxh4 and 2 hxg5 h4 3 ♗d6 ♗f5 are both winning for Black) 2...d4+! 3 exd4 *(2)*.

2) Black to move

3...♔g3! (not 3...♔g4? 4 d5 ♗xd5 5 ♗f2, drawing) 4 ♗a3 (after 4 ♗e7 ♔xh4 5 g6+ ♔g4 Black wins as his bishop can stop both passed pawns on one diagonal) 4...♔xh4 5 ♔d3 ♔xg5 *(3)*.

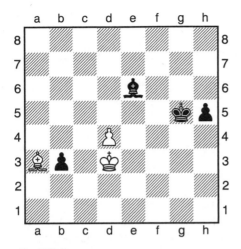

3) White to move

6 ♔e4 h4 7 ♔f3 ♗d5+ and White resigned due to 8 ♔f2 ♔f4 9 ♔g1 h3 10 ♔h2 ♗e6 11 d5 ♗d7 12 ♗b2 ♔e4.

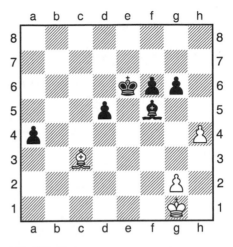

4) Black to move

This is Topalov-Shirov, Linares 1998. Black has only one way to shatter the fortress: 1...♗h3!! (for 1...♗e4? see diagram 6) 2 gxh3 ♔f5 3 ♔f2 ♔e4 *(5)*.

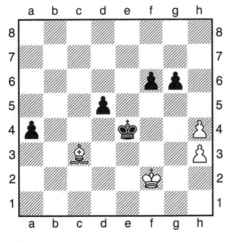

5) White to move

4 ♗xf6 d4 5 ♗e7 ♔d3 6 ♗c5 ♔c4 7 ♗e7 ♔b3 and Topalov resigned due to 8 ♗c5 d3 9 ♔e3 ♔c2 10 ♗b4 a3.

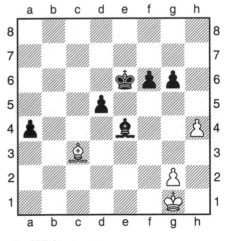

6) White to move

Now White can hold the draw by 2 g3 f5 3 ♔f2 ♔d6 4 ♔e3 ♔c5 5 ♗g7 ♔c4 6 ♗f6 ♔b3 7 ♔d2 ♔a2 8 ♔c1 a3 9 ♗g7. Compare diagram 6 of Lesson 27.

ENDGAME LESSON 29

Bishop against Knight: Advantage for the Bishop

Zugzwang and the lasso

It is an odd coincidence that bishop and knight are of almost equal value on the 8x8 chessboard despite their completely different ways of moving. When they face each other in an endgame, the play and themes are very different, depending on whether it is the bishop or the knight that is playing for a win. Therefore I have split it into two lessons; we start with the bishop playing for a win. Features of the bishop:

1) It is a long-range piece so it profits from an open centre and action on both wings.

2) It thrives in dynamic play, whereas the knight prefers more static situations, where it has time for lengthy manoeuvres.

3) The bishop often profits from fluid pawns, and the knight from broken structures.

4) The knight is more prone to falling into zugzwang. The bishop rarely does, if all its tasks lie on one and the same diagonal.

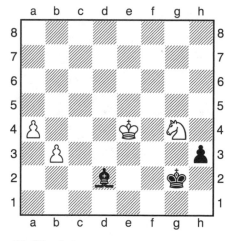

1) Black to move

Black won in Lubbe-Huschenbeth, German Ch, Bad Liebenzell 2010 by using zugzwang again and again: 61...♔g3! 62 ♔f5 ♔f3 63 ♘h2+ ♔g2 64 ♘g4 ♔g3 (2).

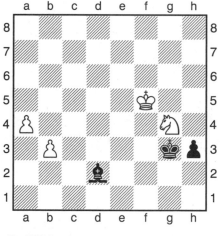

2) White to move

White must now give up one of his pawns due to zugzwang: 65 a5 ♗xa5 66 ♘e3 ♔f2 67 ♘g4+ ♔f3 68 ♔g5 ♔g3 69 ♔h5 (3).

68

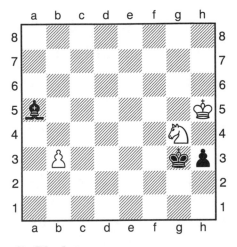

3) Black to move

69...♗d2! (there goes the next) 70 b4 ♗xb4 71 ♘e3 ♗d2 72 ♘f1+ ♚g2 73 ♚g4 ♗g5 0-1. As noted in Lesson 20, knights often struggle versus rook's pawns.

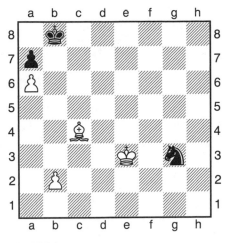

4) White to move

Sometimes the knight can be hunted, like in this position from Sadler-Baramid-ze, Tromsø Olympiad 2014: 51 ♚f4 (51 ♗d3? lets the knight escape by 51...♚c7 52 ♚f4 ♘h5+) 51...♘h5+ *(5)*.

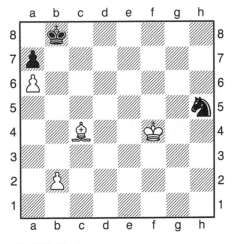

5) White to move

52 ♚g5 ♘g3 (after 52...♘g7 the knight is lassoed by 53 ♗f7 ♚c7 54 ♚f6, winning) 53 ♗d3 *(6)*.

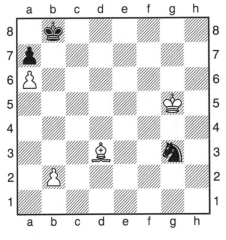

6) Black to move

53...♘h1 (53...♚c7 loses to 54 ♚g4 ♘h1 55 ♚f3) 54 ♚f4 ♘f2 55 ♗c2 and Black resigned as the knight can run but has no way to escape.

Bishop against Knight: Advantage for the Knight

Blinded by the knight

We have just seen some examples of the bishop proving stronger than the knight. As we observed, these pieces are generally speaking of roughly equal value, so the knight naturally has trump cards of its own:

1) The bishop is 'colour-blind' and can visit only half of the squares on the board.

2) Blocked pawns, especially in the centre, can favour the knight.

3) The bishop may be 'bad' (obstructed by its own pawns) and/or have nothing to attack.

4) The knight likes static control, whereas the bishop often profits from dynamics. If there is time, the knight can manoeuvre highly effectively, albeit slowly.

5) While the knight can't lose a tempo to force zugzwang, this task can usually be handled by the attacking king once the knight has established dominance over the position.

Our first diagram below illustrates a typical winning technique.

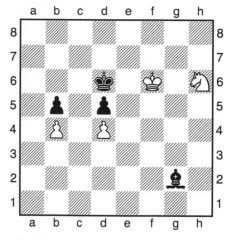

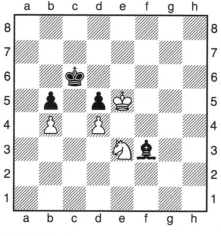

1) White to move

White has full control and the bishop has no active options: 1 ♘f5+ ♚d7 2 ♚e5 ♝f3 3 ♘e3 ♚c6 *(2)*.

2) White to move

4 ♚e6 ♝e2 (4...♝e4 loses to 5 ♘f5) 5 ♘f5 (5 ♘xd5?? backfires completely due to 5...♝c4) 5...♝g4 6 ♚e5 ♝f3 7 ♘e7+ and White wins.

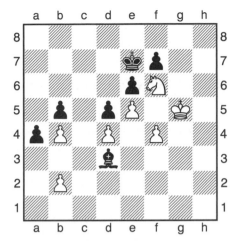

3) White to move

In K.Müller-Bus, Arnhem (junior) 1988, White advanced step by step: 1 ♔h6 ♚f8 2 ♘d7+ ♚g8 3 ♘c5 ♗c2 4 ♔g5 ♚g7 5 ♘a6 ♗d3 6 ♘c7 ♗c4 7 f5 exf5 8 ♔xf5 ♗d3+ *(4)*.

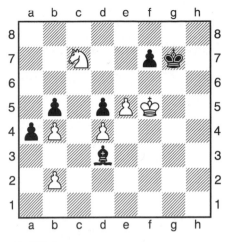

4) White to move

Now comes a triangulation by the king as the knight can't lose a tempo: 9 ♔f4 ♗c4 10 ♔g5 and Black resigned due to the zugzwang.

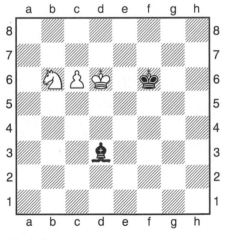

5) White to move

In Anand-Topalov, Monaco (blindfold) 2011, the knight showed its tactical abilities: 66 ♘d7+! *(6)* (not 66 c7? ♗a6, drawing).

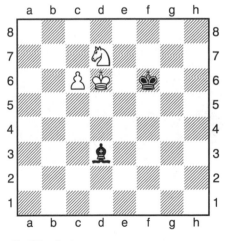

6) Black to move

66...♚g7 (both 66...♚f7 67 ♘e5+ and 66...♚f5 67 ♘c5 are also winning for White) 67 ♘c5 and Black resigned due to 67...♗f5 68 ♚e7 ♗c8 69 ♚d8 ♗f5 70 c7 ♚f7 71 ♘d7.

Rook against Pawn 1

Chess has borrowed bodychecks from ice hockey

Despite the large superiority of a rook over a pawn, this endgame is worth studying as it often arises from rook endings (after a rook sacrifices itself to stop a pawn queening) and there are a few motifs worth knowing:

1) It is possible to defend thanks to stalemate with a knight's pawn on the seventh rank (see diagram 1).

2) Underpromotion to a knight (see diagram 1) can also save the day, provided it is not a rook's pawn. A knight generally draws against a rook (with no pawns), if it is near its king (see Lesson 41).

3) The rook's ability to cut off the defending king is a strong weapon (see diagrams 2 and 3). It wins if, e.g., Black's king is cut off along its fourth rank by White's rook.

4) Bodycheck is by far the most important motif (see diagram 4).

5) Zwischenschach (in-between-check) will be dealt with in the next lesson, together with the avoidance of bodychecks.

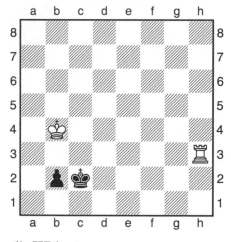

1) White to move

1 ♖h2+ ♔b1!? (Black can also draw by 1...♔c1?! 2 ♔c3 b1♘+! 3 ♔d3 ♘a3 4 ♖a2 ♘b1!) 2 ♔b3 ♔a1! 3 ♖xb2 stalemate.

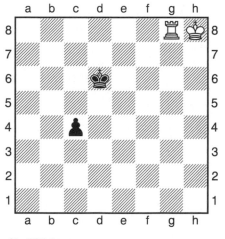

2) White to move

White wins by a cut-off along his fifth rank: 1 ♖g5! c3 (after 1...♔c6 2 ♔g7 White brings in his king) 2 ♖g3 (2 ♖g4?? ♔d5 is only drawn) 2...c2 3 ♖c3 and the pawn is lost.

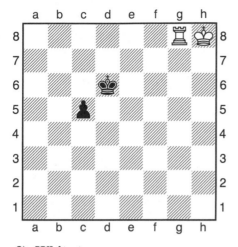

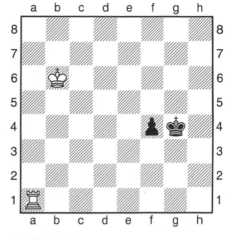

3) White to move

1 ♖g5! (forcing the king to advance on the queenside; 1 ♔g7? runs into the body-check 1...♔e5!!, drawing) 1...♔c6 2 ♔g7 ♔b5 3 ♔f6 ♔b4 4 ♔e5 and White wins.

4) Black to move

Black prepares a bodycheck with a surprising king move: 1...♔f3!! (1...f3? loses to 2 ♔c5 f2 3 ♔d4 ♔f3 4 ♔d3 ♔g2 5 ♔e2) 2 ♔c5 ♔e3! *(5)* (2...♔e2? loses to 3 ♔d4).

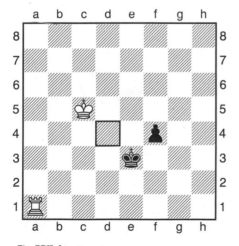

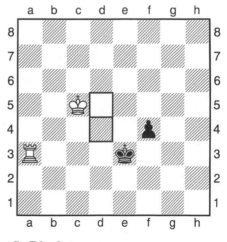

5) White to move

Black's king stops ♔d4. Now 3 ♔d5 f3 4 ♖a3+ ♔e2 5 ♔e4 f2 6 ♖a2+ ♔e1 7 ♔e3 f1♘+ is a draw, while 3 ♖a3+!? *(6)* forces Black to find a precise response.

6) Black to move

3...♔e4! (again Black must give a body-check; 3...♔e2? loses to 4 ♔d4 f3 5 ♖a2+) 4 ♔c4 f3 5 ♖a8 f2 with a draw.

Rook against Pawn 2

Bodycheck avoidance and zwischenschach

As the defending forces consist only of the king and pawn, the bodycheck is the most important motif. Now we shall discuss techniques to *avoid* a bodycheck. Often the attacking king will move to the other side than the defending king (see diagram 1), but sometimes the rook must act first (see diagram 3).

Furthermore, please remember the zwischenschach, which is German for 'in-between check' (see diagram 6) and the right use of the stalemate defence (see diagram 5). Our first position is a famous study by Richard Réti from 1928, where White must avoid bodychecks.

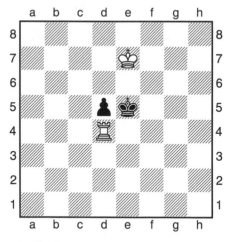

1) White to move

Now the obvious 1 ♖d1? allows Black to draw by 1...d4! 2 ♔d7 ♔d5! 3 ♔c7 ♔c5!! (a bodycheck) 4 ♔b7 ♔c4. Instead White wins with 1 ♖d2 d4 2 ♖d1 (zugzwang) 2...♔d5 *(2)*.

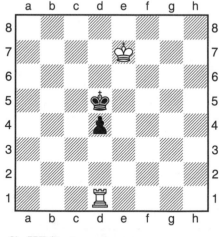

2) White to move

3 ♔d7 (but not 3 ♔f6? ♔e4!, drawing) 3...♔c4 4 ♔d6 d3 5 ♔e5 (White's king moves to the other side, thus avoiding a bodycheck) 5...♔c3 6 ♔e4 d2 7 ♔e3 and White wins.

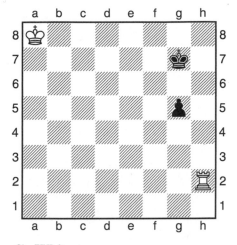

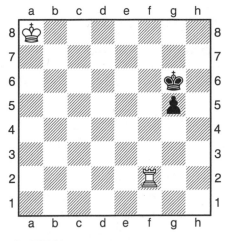

3) White to move

1 ♔b7? ♔f6 2 ♔c6 runs into the body-check 2...♔e5!, drawing. In Lerner-Dorf-man, Tashkent 1980, White found the only winning move: 1 ♖f2!! (bodycheck avoid-ance) 1...♔g6 *(4)*.

4) White to move

Only now can the king move in: 2 ♔b7 g4 3 ♔c6 ♔g5 4 ♔d5 g3 5 ♖f8 ♔g4 6 ♔e4 1-0.

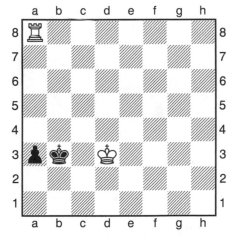

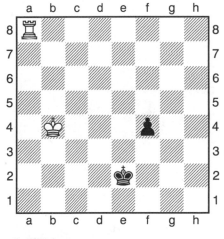

5) Black to move

Here 1...a2? loses to 2 ♖b8+ ♔a3 3 ♔c2 a1♘+ 4 ♔c3. Black draws by 1...♔b2! 2 ♖b8+ ♔c1 3 ♖a8 ♔b2 4 ♔d2 a2 5 ♖b8+ ♔a1 6 ♔c2 stalemate.

6) White to move

1 ♔c3? allows Black to draw by 1...f3 2 ♖e8+ ♔d1. Only the zwischenschach 1 ♖e8+ wins: 1...♔d2 2 ♖f8 ♔e3 3 ♔c3 f3 4 ♖e8+ ♔f2 5 ♔d2.

Rook against Pawns

The king comes first

The motifs are similar to that of the previous two lessons on rook against pawn. The new element is that the side with the pawns can also play for a win, if they are far-advanced. In particular, two connected passed pawns on their sixth rank generally beat a lone rook.

The rook on the other hand has a standard way to deal with far-advanced pawns. For this, see diagram 3, which is based on an example by Sozin, who put White's king on a7. If the king can help the far-advanced connected passed pawns then diagram 5 shows an important technique. Again the king must move in first.

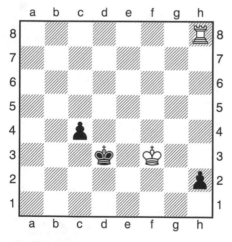

1) White to move

66 罝xh2? runs into 66...c3 67 罝h8 c2 68 罝c8 含d2, drawing. In Leko-Markowski, Polanica Zdroj 1998 White won with 66 含f2!! (the king comes first) 66...含d2 *(2)*.

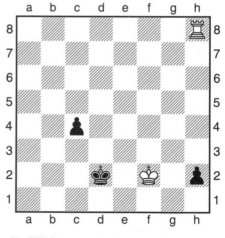

2) White to move

Now the pawn can be taken: 67 罝xh2 c3 68 含f1+ 含d1 (68...含d3 69 含e1 c2 70 罝h3+ and White wins) 69 罝h8 c2 70 罝d8+ 含c1 71 含e2 1-0.

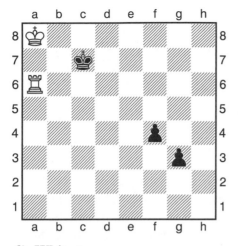

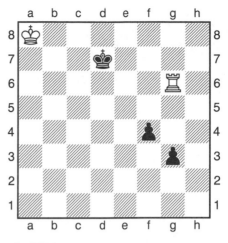

3) White to move

Now the rook must move behind the more advanced passed pawn: 1 ♖g6! (not 1 ♔a7? f3 – two connected passed pawns on their sixth rank almost always overpower a rook) 1...♔d7 *(4)*.

4) White to move

2 ♖g4! g2 (2...♔e6 loses to 3 ♖xf4 ♔e5 4 ♖g4) 3 ♖xg2 ♔e6 4 ♖g5! (an important cut-off – see diagram 2 of Lesson 31) 4...♔f6 5 ♖a5 and White wins.

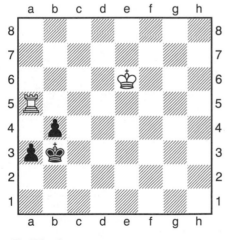

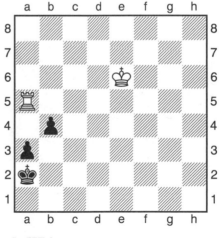

5) Black to move

60...a2? throws away the win: 61 ♔d5 ♔b2 62 ♔c4 b3 63 ♖a8 draws. In Parligras-Gopal, Gibraltar 2012, Black advanced his king first: 60...♔a2! *(6)*.

6) White to move

Black wins after 61 ♔d5 b3 62 ♔c4 b2 63 ♖b5 b1♕ 64 ♖xb1 ♔xb1 65 ♔b3 a2, while the game ended 61 ♖h5 b3 62 ♔d5 b2 63 ♖h2 ♔a1 0-1.

ENDGAME LESSON 34

Rook Endings 1: Understanding the Basics

The foundation of endgame theory

Rook endings occur often in practical play and there are several really important positions and guidelines that you need to know. Rook endings have a relatively large drawish tendency and so we start with two of the main drawing positions. Philidor's is the most important as it can be applied often and is the main reason why the endgame rook and pawn vs rook is usually drawn if the defending king manages to get in front of the pawn. The idea is that the defending rook moves to the rank in front of the pawn. The attacker can only make progress by advancing the pawn, but then the attacking king has no shelter against rook checks from behind. In diagram 1 this is explained in detail; the configuration could be moved across almost the whole board and the defender could draw in a similar way. In Karstedt's draw (see diagram 5) the defending rook moves behind the pawn and the defending king to the 'short' side of the pawn, so that the rook has enough checking distance from the 'long' side.

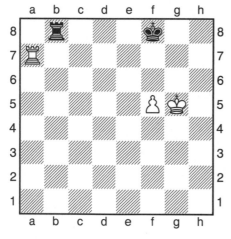

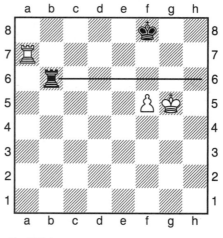

1) Black to move

If Black is to play, he draws easily with 1...♖b6!?; e.g., 2 ♖h7 ♖a6 3 ♖h8+ (3 ♖h6 ♖xh6 4 ♔xh6 ♔f7 is a drawn pawn ending) 3...♔f7 4 ♖b8 ♖c6 5 ♖b7+ ♔f8 6 ♖a7 ♖b6 *(2)*.

2) White to move

White is unable to make progress without advancing the pawn, but 7 f6 is met by 7...♖b1 8 ♔g6 ♖g1+, when White's king has no shelter from the checks.

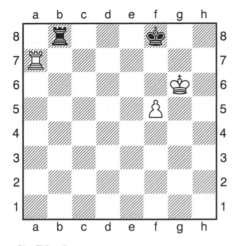

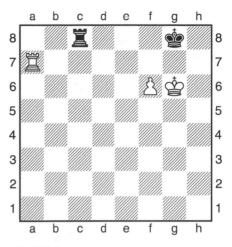

3) Black to move

Here White has been able to play ♔g6 before Black could put his rook on his third rank. White now wins: 1...♖c8 (1...♖b1 loses to 2 ♖a8+ ♔e7 3 f6+ ♔e6 4 ♖e8+ ♔d7 5 f7) 2 f6 ♔g8!? *(4)*.

4) White to move

3 ♖h7?! makes no progress owing to 3...♖c6!, but the zwischenschach 3 ♖g7+! wins for White: 3...♔h8 4 ♖h7+ ♔g8 5 f7+ or 3...♔f8 4 ♖h7 ♔g8 5 f7+.

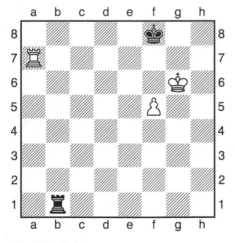

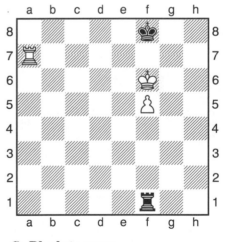

5) Black to move

Black should play 1...♖f1!? (1...♖g1+?! 2 ♔f6 ♔g8 3 ♖a8+ ♔h7 4 ♔f7 ♖b1 draws as well; for 1...♖b6+? 2 f6 see diagram 3) 2 ♔f6 *(6)*.

6) Black to move

2...♔g8! (moving to the 'short' side of the pawn; for 2...♔e8?, losing to 3 ♖a8+ ♔d7 4 ♖f8, see the next lesson) 3 ♖a8+ ♔h7 and both 4 ♔e6 ♔g7 and 4 ♖f8 ♖a1! 5 ♖e8 ♖f1 6 ♖e5 ♔g8 are drawn.

35 Rook Endings 2: Miraculous Draws?

Drawn – just as Tarrasch said!

Here we take a look at some important positions that look desperate for the defender, but are nevertheless drawn, in keeping with Tarrasch's famous aphorism that "all rook endings are drawn". This is not, of course, the case and the next lesson will describe the most important win ('Lucena'). This lesson deals with the passive defence against a knight's pawn, the defence on the back rank and Tarrasch's drawing position, which is based on the defence on the back rank. Especially important is the only drawing move 1...♔g6!! in diagram 4 as the rook must maintain the critical three-squares checking distance. Our first position shows why even passive defence holds against a knight's pawn: the attacking rook does not have enough space on the kingside.

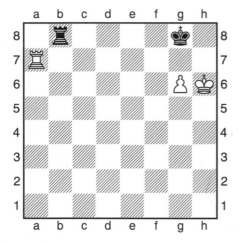

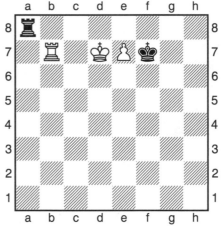

1) White to move

1 ♖g7+ ♔h8! (1...♔f8?? loses to 2 ♔h7! ♖b1 3 ♖f7+ ♔e8 4 ♔g8 – see Lesson 36) 2 ♖h7+ ♔g8 with a draw.

2) Black to move

Even this is a draw: 1...♖e8! (1...♖h8?? 2 ♖b1 is a win for White) 2 ♔d6 ♖a8!, etc. (2...♖g8? loses to 3 ♖b4; 2...♔f6? 3 ♖b3 and White wins after 3...♖xe7 4 ♖f3+ or 3...♖a8 4 ♖f3+ ♔g7 5 ♖a3!).

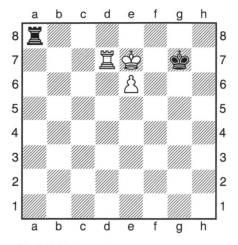

3) White to move

Tarrasch's draw is based on a defence on the back rank: 1 罝b7 (for 1 罝d6 see diagram 4) 1...含g6 2 含d6 含f6 3 e7 含f7 4 含d7 罝e8, holding the draw.

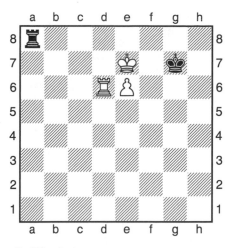

4) Black to move

1...含g6!! (both 1...罝a1? 2 含e8! and 1...罝a7+? 2 含e8! 罝a8+ 3 罝d8! 罝a6 4 e7 罝a7 5 罝c8 含f6 6 罝c6+! are lost for Black, while for 1...罝b8?, see diagram 6) 2 罝c6 (5).

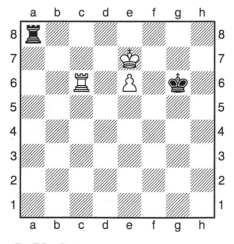

5) Black to move

Again the king must move as Black's rook is optimally placed on a8: 2...含g7! 3 罝c7 含g6 4 罝b7 含g7 5 罝d7 含g6, and White can make no progress.

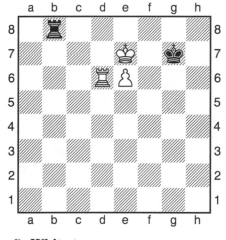

6) White to move

Now the checking distance is too short: 2 罝d8 罝b7+ 3 含d6 罝b6+ 4 含d7 罝b7+ 5 含c6 罝e7 6 含d6 含f6 7 罝f8+ and White wins.

Rook Endings 3: Winning with Lucena

The mother of many winning positions

Philidor's position is the foundation of many draws and Lucena's win is the fundamental winning position for which the attacker aims. It applies if he can get his king in front of the pawn and the defending king is cut off to the side. It works for all pawns on the seventh rank except a rook's pawn, which will be dealt with later (see Lesson 38). The winning manoeuvre is also called 'building a bridge' as the rook moves in closer to shelter the attacking king from checks. The resulting picture looks like a bridge, with White's king and rook being the pillar in the middle. Diagram 3 is also very important since you should know how to reach the Lucena position from there.

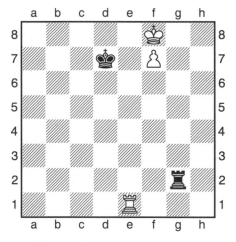

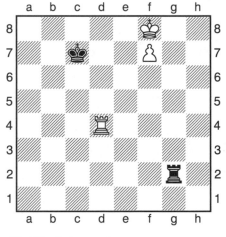

1) White to move

First the king is forced away: 1 ♖d1+ ♔c7 (1...♔e6 2 ♔e8 and 1...♔c6 2 ♖d4 ♔c5 3 ♖d7 ♔c6 4 ♔e8 ♖f2 5 ♖e7 are also winning for White) 2 ♖d4 *(2)*.

2) Black to move

The rook moves to this precise square to provide shelter for the white king. 2...♖g1 3 ♔e7 ♖e1+ 4 ♔f6 ♖f1+ 5 ♔e6 ♖e1+ (5...♖f2 loses to 6 ♖d5) 6 ♔f5 ♖f1+ 7 ♖f4 and White wins – that's why the rook moved to the fourth rank.

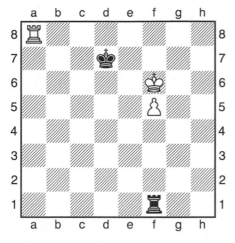

3) White to move

1 ♖f8!? (White's rook must be used in both directions; after 1 ♔g6?? ♔e7! Black reaches Karstedt's draw – see diagram 5 of Lesson 34) 1...♖f2 *(4)*.

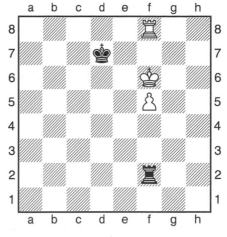

4) White to move

After 2 ♔g7, both 2...♔e7 3 f6+ ♔e6 4 ♖e8+ and 2...♖g2+ 3 ♔f7 ♖f2 4 f6 ♖f1 5 ♖a8 ♖f2 6 ♔g7 ♖g2+ 7 ♔f8 ♖f2 8 f7 are winning for White.

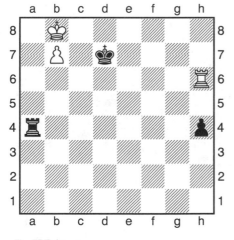

5) White to move

Sometimes even a defending pawn does not help, as in Topalov-Karpov, Cannes 2002: 70 ♖h7+ ♔d8 *(6)* (70...♔d6 loses to 71 ♔c8 ♖c4+ 72 ♔d8 ♖b4 73 ♖h6+).

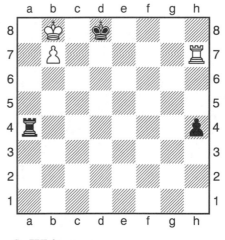

6) White to move

After 71 ♖h8+ ♔d7 72 ♖h6 White has lost a tempo and Black falls into a fatal zugzwang: 72...♔d8 73 ♖h7 ♖b4 74 ♔a7 ♖a4+ 75 ♔b6 1-0.

Rook Endings 4:
Ways to Cut the King Off

Horizontal cut-offs are even better than vertical ones

Endgame analysts have deeply investigated positions with rook and pawn vs rook where the defending king is cut off from the pawn but a Lucena-type position has not yet been reached. We start with vertical cut-offs along a file. If the attacking pawn has crossed the middle of the board then the attacker usually wins, if there is no immediate draw. The most interesting situation is with the pawn on its fourth rank. Then there are two main cases:

1) If the defending king is cut off by two files, then the attacker wins, as long as the pawn is a centre pawn or a bishop's pawn. Diagram 3 shows how to defend against a knight's pawn.

2) If the defending king is cut off by one file, the position is usually drawn – see diagram 1.

A horizontal cut-off is usually even better for the attacker. This is because the rook can shield the attacking king from the checks and can protect the advancing pawn – see diagram 5, which was analysed by Tarrasch in 1908.

The rook's pawn is a special case – see the next lesson.

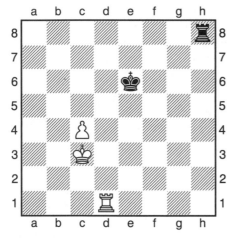

1) White to move

1 ♔b4 (1 c5 ♔e7 2 ♔c4 ♖d8 is a draw) 1...♖b8+ (Black's rook has three squares' checking distance, which is enough) 2 ♔a5 *(2)*.

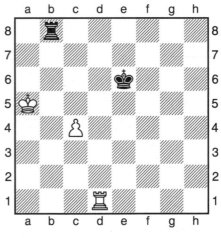

2) Black to move

2...♖c8! (after 2...♖a8+? White is able to shorten the checking distance by 3 ♔b6!, winning) 3 ♔b5 ♖b8+ 4 ♔a6 ♖c8 5 ♖d4 ♔e5! 6 ♖d5+ ♔e6, with a draw.

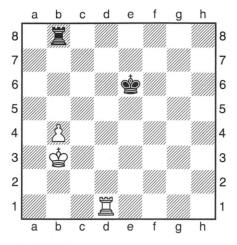

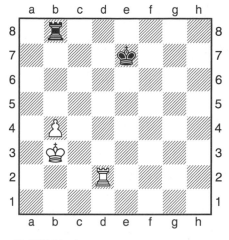

3) White to move

1 ♖d2 ♚e5! (for 1...♚e7? see diagram 4) 2 ♔c4 ♖c8+ 3 ♔b5 ♖b8+ 4 ♔c5 ♖c8+ 5 ♔b6 ♖b8+ 6 ♔a5 ♖a8+ 7 ♔b5 ♖b8+ 8 ♔a4 ♖a8+ 9 ♔b3 ♖b8, and Black holds the draw.

4) White to move

White wins with a very precise manoeuvre: 2 ♖d4! ♚e6 3 ♔c4! ♖c8+ 4 ♔b5 ♚e5 5 ♖h4 ♚d6 6 ♖h6+ ♚d7 7 ♖h7+ ♚d6 8 ♔a6 ♖a8+ 9 ♔b7.

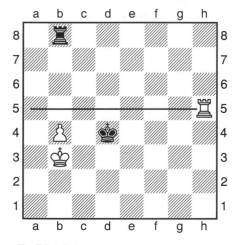

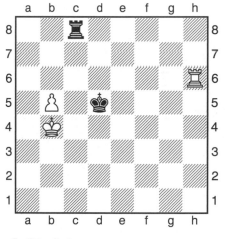

5) Black to move

White wins easily: 1...♖c8 2 b5 ♖c5 3 ♖h4+ ♚d5 4 ♔b4 ♖c8 5 ♖h6 (6) (again using the horizontal cut-off).

6) Black to move

5...♖c1 6 ♔a5 ♖a1+ 7 ♔b6 ♖b1 8 ♔a6 ♖a1+ 9 ♔b7 ♖g1 10 b6 ♚c5 11 ♔a7 ♖a1+ 12 ♔b8 ♖a6 13 ♔c7 and White wins.

85

Rook Endings 5:
Rook's Pawns are Different

Vančura's draw with rook and rook's pawn

The drawing margin is even larger with rook and rook's pawn vs rook. The most 'miraculous' draw in practice is Vančura's famous position – refer to diagram 2 to see the idea in a nutshell.

The attacker really needs a large advantage if he is to win. The defending king must be cut off very far away – see diagram 3. In diagram 5 the attacking rook is used as a shield so that the attacker can win by cutting off the defending king horizontally.

We start off in diagram 1 with the Vančura draw. Black's king waits on g7 and h7, while the rook on f6 maintains an attack on the a6-pawn, forcing the white rook to stay in front of it. If White pushes his pawn to a7, then the black rook can switch to attacking it from behind. White's king has nowhere to hide from checks on the queenside, so he has no way to win.

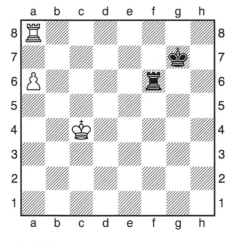

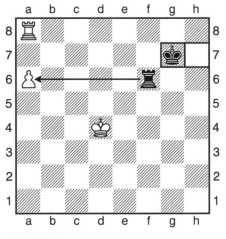

1) White to move

After 1 ♔b5 ♖f5+ 2 ♔b6 ♖f6+ 3 ♔c5 (3 ♔b7 ♖f7+ allows the king no hiding place) 3...♖f5+ 4 ♔d4 ♖f6!! *(2)* Black maintains the Vančura set-up.

2) White to move

5 ♖a7+ ♔g6 6 ♔e5 ♖b6 7 ♖a8 ♔g7 (7...♔f7? loses to 8 a7 ♖a6 9 ♖h8 ♖xa7 10 ♖h7+) 8 ♔d5 ♖f6 9 a7 ♖a6 (now the rook goes behind the pawn) 10 ♔c5 ♖a1, with a draw.

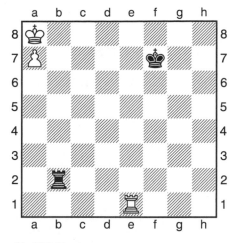

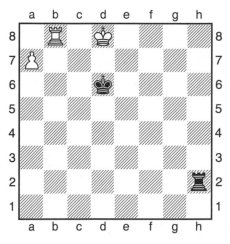

3) White to move

For White to win, the black king must be cut off by *four* files. 1 罝c1 含e7 2 罝c8 含d6!? (2...含d7 loses to 3 罝b8 罝a2 4 含b7 罝b2+ 5 含a6) 3 罝b8 罝a2 4 含b7 罝b2+ 5 含c8 罝c2+ 6 含d8 罝h2 *(4)*.

4) White to move

Now a tactical trick does the job: 7 罝b6+! 含c5 8 罝c6+ 含xc6 (8...含d5 9 罝a6 and 8...含b5 9 罝c8 are also winning for White) 9 a8豐+ 含c5 10 豐c8+ 含d4 11 豐g4+ and White wins.

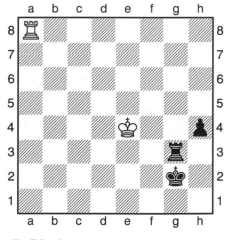

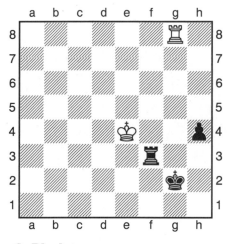

5) Black to move

Black used his rook as a shield in Lautier-Salov, Madrid 1993: 1...罝f3!! (and not 1...h3? 2 罝a2+ 含g1 3 含f4 罝g2 4 罝a1+ 含h2 5 含f3, with a draw) 2 罝g8+ *(6)*.

6) Black to move

2...含f2 3 罝a8 h3 4 罝a7 含g2 (4...h2?? allows 5 罝a2+ 含g3 6 罝xh2, drawing) 5 罝h7 罝g3 0-1.

ENDGAME LESSON 39

Rook Endings 6: Rooks and Passed Pawns

The rook belongs behind a passed pawn – whether friend or foe

"Put rooks behind passed pawns!" is a useful guideline; while it shouldn't be applied blindly, in most cases it holds true. By placing our rook behind our own passed pawn, we threaten a decisive advance of the pawn. If the defending rook must simply blockade the pawn, this can leave it totally passive, whereas our own rook remains active. Conversely, by placing our rook behind an enemy passed pawn, we make it harder for the pawn to advance. If the enemy rook is forced in front of its pawn, our opponent might be able to advance the pawn as far as the seventh rank, but then find there is no way to finish the job by promoting the pawn, as it is blocked by the rook. Diagram 3 from Djokić-Trifunović, Kraljevo 2011, shows another important case where the attacking rook belongs behind the pawn. Often the attacker queens too early in such situations. Diagram 5, from John-Alekhine, Hamburg 1910, is an instance where the standard guideline is best ignored. But in our first example, from Kariakin-Nisipeanu, Medias 2011, White's rook indeed belongs behind the passed a-pawn.

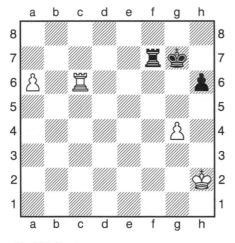

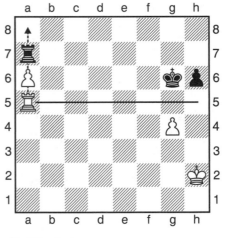

1) White to move

65 ♖c2! (65 ♖c3? allows Black's rook to get behind the passed pawn: 65...♖f2+! 66 ♔g3 ♖a2, drawing) 65...♖a7 (the game ended 65...h5 66 ♖a2 1-0) 66 ♖a2 ♔g6 67 ♖a5! *(2)*.

2) Black to move

The rook completely dominates Black. 67...♔f6 68 ♔g3 ♔g6 69 ♔f4 ♔f6 70 ♔e4 ♔g6 (70...♔e6 71 ♖h5) 71 ♔d4 ♔f6 72 ♔c5 and White wins.

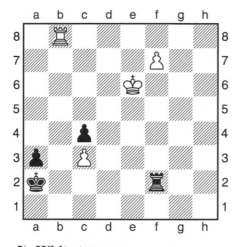

3) White to move

62 f8♕? (White rushes; the typical 62 ♖b5! wins after 62...♖xf7 63 ♔xf7 ♔a1 64 ♖b4 or 62...♔a1 63 ♖f5) 62...♖xf8 63 ♖xf8 ♔b3 *(4)*.

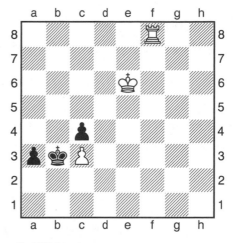

4) White to move

64 ♔d5 (64 ♖a8 a2 65 ♖xa2 is met by 65...♔xc3!!, drawing) 64...♔xc3 65 ♖f3+ ♔b2 66 ♔xc4 a2 67 ♖f2+ ♔a3! 68 ♖f3+ ♔b2 69 ♖f2+ ♔a3 70 ♖f1 ♔b2 ½-½.

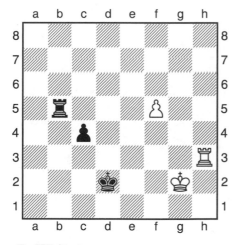

5) White to move

54 ♖f3? (White commits the rook too early; 54 f6 keeps it flexible, and White draws after 54...♖f5 55 ♖f3 or 54...c3 55 ♖h8 ♖f5 56 ♖d8+ ♔c1 57 ♖d6) 54...c3 *(6)*.

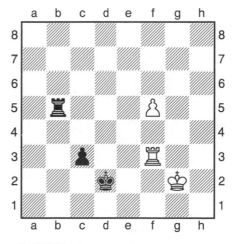

6) White to move

55 ♖f2+ ♔d3 56 ♖f3+ ♔d4 57 f6 c2 58 f7 c1♕ 59 f8♕ ♕d2+ (with so much fire-power on the board and exposed kings, the first check is often decisive) 60 ♖f2 ♕g5+ 61 ♔h3 ♕h5+ 62 ♔g3 ♖g5+ 0-1.

Rook Endings 7:
Good Attackers, Poor Defenders

Activate the rook!

An active rook is a very powerful force and this is one of the reasons for the large drawish tendency of rook endings. If the defender can activate his rook even at the cost of a pawn, he may well have good drawing chances. It also explains why the defending king should blockade passed pawns and not the rook.

As a rule, passive defence is the wrong approach in positions with many static weaknesses. So in diagram 1 Black should activate his rook sooner rather than later and switch the roles of the defending pieces: the black king must defend the queenside while the rook aims for active counterplay. In diagram 2 the picture has changed. Such an active rook can only rarely be defeated. In diagram 3 Flohr shows a typical way to open roads as his attacking pieces are more mobile than Black's.

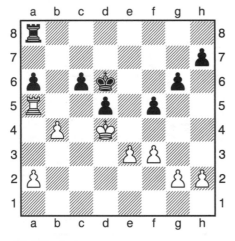

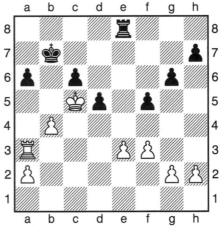

1) Black to move

This is the classic game Flohr-Vidmar, Nottingham 1936. 36...♔c7! (36...♖b8? 37 a3 ♖a8 was played in the game – see diagram 3) 37 ♔c5 ♔b7 38 ♖a3 ♖e8 *(2)*.

2) White to move

39 ♔d6 g5 and Black draws after 40 g3 g4 41 fxg4 fxg4 42 ♖c3 ♖f8 or 40 ♖c3 f4 41 exf4 gxf4, as Dvoretsky indicates.

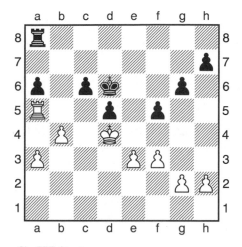

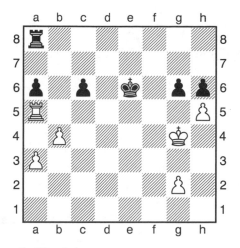

3) White to move

38 e4! fxe4 39 fxe4 dxe4 40 ♔xe4 ♖a7? (40...♖c7 is again called for) 41 ♔f4 h6 42 h4 ♔e6 43 ♔g4 ♖a8 44 h5 *(4)*.

4) Black to move

44...g5? (the rook had to be activated with 44...♖g8! now) 45 g3 ♖a7 46 ♔f3 ♖a8 47 ♔e4 ♖a7 48 ♔d4 ♔d6 49 ♔e4 ♔e6 *(5)*.

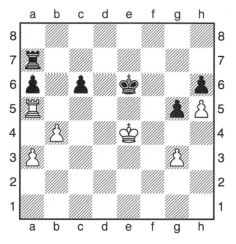

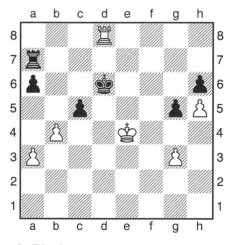

5) White to move

50 ♖e5+ ♔d6 (50...♔f6 51 ♖c5 ♖c7 52 ♖a5 ♖a7 53 ♔d4 is also winning for White) 51 ♖e8 c5 52 ♖d8+ *(6)*.

6) Black to move

52...♔c6 (Flohr analysed 52...♔c7 53 ♖h8 cxb4 54 ♖h7+ ♔b6 55 ♖xa7 ♔xa7 56 axb4, when White wins) 53 ♖c8+ ♔b6 54 ♖xc5 ♖h7 55 ♔e5 ♔c6 56 ♖e6+ ♔b5 57 ♔f5 ♖f7+ 58 ♖f6 1-0.

41 Rook against Knight (no Pawns)

Knight check shadows and other knightmares

Although a rook is a good deal more powerful than a knight, this ending is usually a draw if the knight is within reach of the defending king, even when they are at the edge of the board. But problems can arise from two sources:

1) If the king and knight are permanently separated, then the rook usually wins (see diagram 1). There are typical domination distances, which you should know, like the knight check shadow, when attacking king and knight are separated by one square diagonally, e.g. white ♔e4 vs black ♞g6.

2) If the knight is on an unfortunate square like a1 or b2 (or the analogous squares in other corners; see also diagram 5 of Lesson 32) then the rook has good chances to win (diagram 6 shows a case in point). This was already known to the Arabic endgame theorists 1000 years ago since back then the king, rook and knight already moved in the same way that they do today.

In diagram 1, the knight can be hunted, dominated and won.

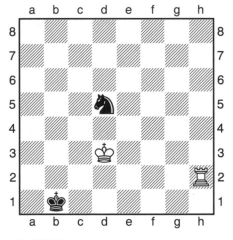

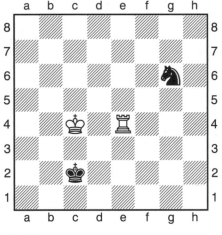

1) White to move

In the game Musalov-Shukh, Taganrog 2011, White went astray with 67 ♖f2? – see diagram 3. He can win as follows: 67 ♖h4 ♔b2 68 ♖d4 ♞e7 69 ♔c4 ♔c2 70 ♖f4 ♞g6 71 ♖e4 *(2)*.

2) Black to move

Domination! 71...♔d2 72 ♔d4 ♞f8 73 ♖e8 ♞h7 74 ♖g8 ♞f6 75 ♖g7 ♔e2 76 ♔e5 ♞h5 77 ♖g5 and White wins.

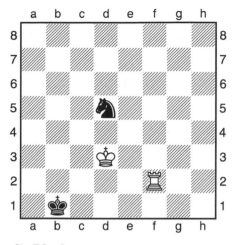

3) Black to move

The game continued 67...♞b4+ 68 ♔c4 ♞a2 69 ♔b3 ♞c1+ 70 ♔a3 ♞d3 71 ♖d2 ♞c1 72 ♖b2+ ♔a1 73 ♖b8 ♞a2? *(4)* (for 73...♞e2! see diagram 5).

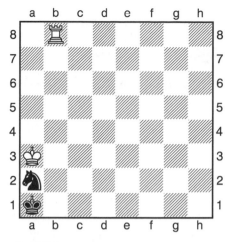

4) White to move

White now won as follows: 74 ♔b3 ♔b1 75 ♖b7 ♞c1+ 76 ♔c3+ ♔a1 77 ♔c2 ♞a2 78 ♖b1# (1-0).

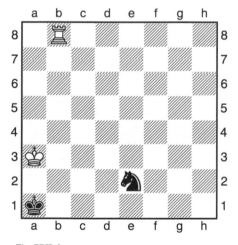

5) White to move

Black draws after 74 ♔b3 ♔b1 or 74 ♖e8 ♞c1 75 ♖d8 ♔b1 76 ♖d2 ♔a1 77 ♖b2 ♞d3 78 ♖d2 ♞c1.

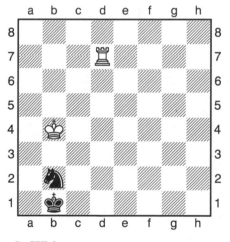

6) White to move

The neatest win is 1 ♔a3 ♔a1 2 ♔b3 ♔b1 3 ♖d2 ♔a1 4 ♖h2. Instead, 1 ♔b3?! is met by 1...♔c1 2 ♖c7+ ♔b1 3 ♔c3, when White can win, but it takes much longer.

ENDGAME LESSON 42 Rook against Knight (with Pawns)

Fortresses can be broken by zugzwang and invasions

Once we add some pawns on both sides, the difference in strength between the rook and the knight is far more likely to produce a decisive result. When there are open lines and pawns to take or support, the rook is greatly superior to the slow-moving and sometimes clumsy knight.

Assuming the player with the knight doesn't have a major compensating advantage (such as a couple of extra pawns!) or chances to eliminate the last enemy pawn, his main hope lies in either creating dangerous passed pawns or else constructing a fortress. We shall focus on the latter possibility. If the knight only needs to defend a limited front, then the rook's great ability to manoeuvre across the whole board may prove irrelevant. Usually a purely passive defence is insufficient; the knight needs to have some sort of target to tie down the enemy king or rook. Zugzwang is one of the main weapons for the player with the rook.

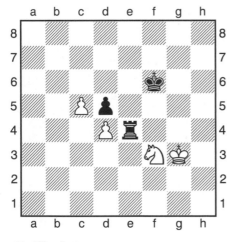

1) Black to move

In the game Pert-Flear, British League 2009/10, Black triangulated: 50...♚f5 51 ♘h4+ ♚g5 52 ♘f3+ ♚f6 53 ♚f2 (53 c6 loses to 53...♚e7) 53...♚f5 *(2)*.

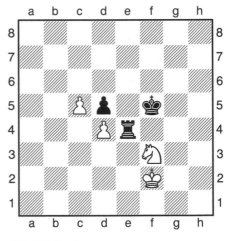

2) White to move

54 c6 (54 ♚g3 ♖e3 55 ♚f2 ♚e4 is winning for Black) 54...♖e8 55 ♘e5?! (for 55 ♘d2 see diagram 4) 55...♚e4 *(3)*.

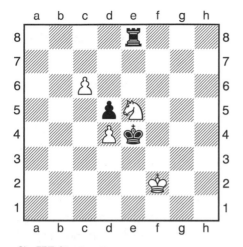

3) White to move

56 c7 (56 ♘g6 loses to 56...♔xd4 57 c7 ♖c8) 56...♖c8 57 ♘f7 ♖xc7 58 ♘d6+ ♔d3 59 ♔f3 ♖d7 60 ♘f5 ♖f7 0-1.

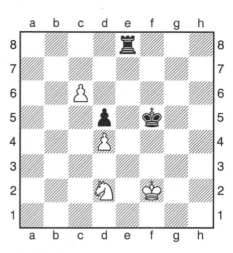

4) Black to move

55...♔f4 (55...♖c8? 56 ♔f3 ♖xc6 57 ♘f1 ♖c3+ 58 ♘e3+ leads to a typical fortress draw) 56 ♘b3 ♖c8 57 ♘c5 ♖xc6 *(5).*

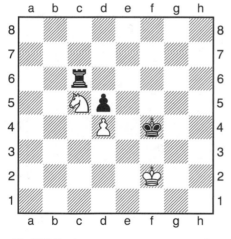

5) White to move

White's knight can't reach c3 or e3 (where it would tie Black down to defending d5) in time so Black wins: 58 ♔e2 ♖h6 59 ♔d3 ♖h3+ 60 ♔d2 ♖a3 61 ♔e2 *(6).*

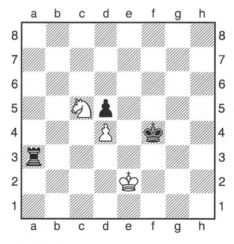

6) Black to move

61...♖a2+ 62 ♔d3 ♔f3 63 ♘b7 ♖a1 64 ♘d6 ♖a3+ 65 ♔d2 ♖b3 66 ♔c2 ♖b6 67 ♘f5 ♔e4 and Black wins.

43 Rook against Bishop (no Pawns)

The safe corner and the shadow of the kings

Usually the pawnless endgame of rook vs bishop is drawn. However, it is important to be aware of which corners are 'safe' for the bishop – perhaps a little paradoxically, they are the ones where the bishop *cannot* cover the corner square. The point is that he is then saved by stalemate ideas with the king in the corner square and the bishop on the square next to the king (see diagram 1). However, even near the 'safe' corner, some care is needed to achieve the drawing set-up. The main problems arise when the defending king is caught near the corner that the bishop *can* control; this is the 'dangerous' corner in this type of endgame (see diagram 3, which is from Breyer-Tarrasch, Berlin 1920). In diagram 6 (from Radjabov-Ivanchuk, Khanty-Mansiisk 2011), the king is in-between the corners, and the bishop succeeds in preventing the approach of the enemy king on a relatively long diagonal.

Our first example features the defence in the safe corner and the most dangerous trap against it.

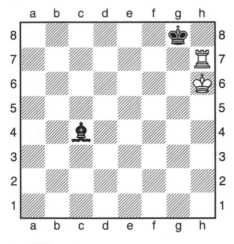

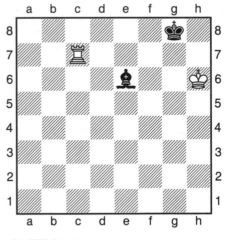

1) White to move

56 ♖c7 ♗b3 (for 56...♗e6? see diagram 2) 57 ♔g6 ♔h8 58 ♖c8+ ♔g8 59 ♖c1 ♗h7+ 60 ♔f6 ♗g8 61 ♖c2 ♗h7 and Black holds the draw.

2) White to move

Sachdev-Schut, Wijk aan Zee 2012 concluded 57 ♔g6 ♔h8 (57...♗h3!? loses to 58 ♖e7 ♔f8 59 ♖e5) 58 ♖h7+ ♔g8 59 ♖e7 1-0.

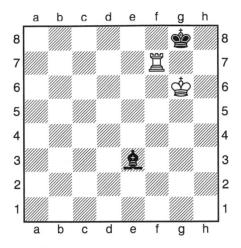

3) Black to move

After 1...♗g1 2 ♖f1 ♗h2 3 ♖h1 ♗g3 4 ♖h3 *(4)* the rook forces the bishop to leave the 'shadow' of the kings.

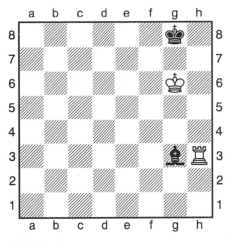

4) Black to move

4...♗d6 (White also wins after 4...♗f4 5 ♖c3 ♔f8 6 ♖f3, 4...♗f2 5 ♖a3 ♔f8 6 ♖f3+ or 4...♗e5 5 ♖e3 ♗d6 6 ♖e8+ ♗f8 7 ♖a8 ♔h8 8 ♖xf8#) 5 ♖d3 *(5)*.

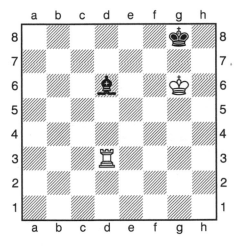

5) Black to move

5...♗c7 loses to 6 ♖c3 ♔d8 7 ♖c8, while after 5...♗e7 6 ♖c3 Black resigned due to 6...♔f8 7 ♖c8+ ♗d8 8 ♖xd8+.

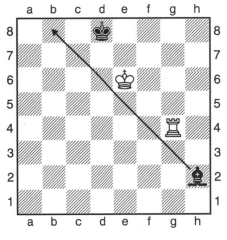

6) White to move

Black's bishop controls the b8-h2 diagonal; after 98 ♖g7 ♔c8 99 ♖d7 ♗c7 100 ♖d3 Black played 100...♗b8 (100...♗h2 is also good) and went on to draw.

ENDGAME LESSON 44 — Rook against Bishop (with Pawns)

The pawns often complement the bishop

The bishop is a long-range piece and so has better chances vs a rook than the knight had (see Lesson 42), but it is still at a severe disadvantage. With pawns on both wings, the rook is far superior and has very good winning chances. But much depends on colour complexes and the interplay between the bishop and the pawn-structures.

For many players it seems natural that the defending pawns should be put on the same-coloured squares as the bishop so that it can protect them. But this is often wrong as the enemy king can then penetrate on the other colour complex and he often wins by domination and zugzwang – see diagram 3, which is from Real de Azua-Coppola, Montevideo 2011.

If the bishop can attack the enemy pawn(s), its prospects are better, and diagram 1 (from analysis by Averbakh of the game Rubinstein-Tartakower, Vienna 1922) is indeed drawn. Diagram 5 shows the most important fortress of the whole endgame.

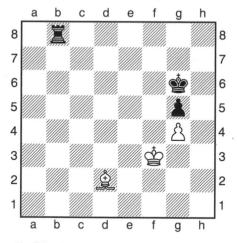

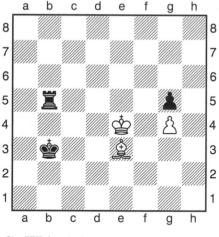

1) Black to move

The g5-pawn must be kept guarded by either king or rook. 1...♖b5 2 ♔e4 ♔f6 3 ♗c3+ ♔e6 4 ♗d2 ♔d6 5 ♗e3 ♔c6 6 ♗d2 ♔b6 7 ♗e3+ ♔a5 8 ♗d2+ ♔a4 9 ♗e3 ♔b3 *(2)*.

2) White to move

10 ♗c1 (10 ♗xg5? loses to 10...♖xg5 11 ♔f4 ♖g8 12 g5 ♔c4 13 ♔f5 ♔d5) 10...♔c2 11 ♗xg5 ♖xg5 12 ♔f4, with a draw. Compare Lessons 31 and 32.

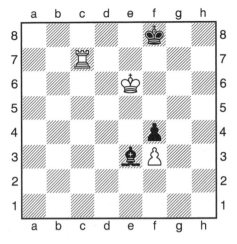

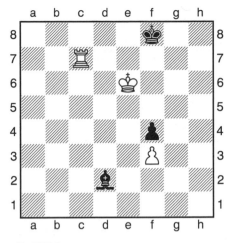

3) White to move

74 ♖f7+ ♚e8 75 ♖d7 ♚f8 76 ♖c7 (the typical zugzwang) 76...♗d4?! (for the alternative 76...♗d2 see the next diagram) 77 ♖f7+ 1-0.

4) White to move

77 ♚f6 wins after 77...♚e8 78 ♖e7+ ♚d8 79 ♖e4 or 77...♚g8 78 ♖g7+ ♚f8 79 ♖d7 ♗c3+ 80 ♚f5 ♚e8 81 ♖d3.

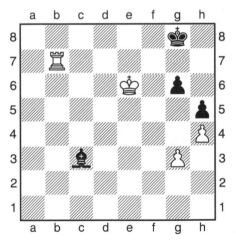

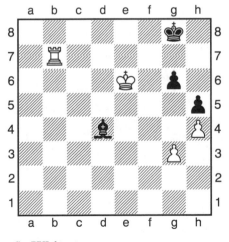

5) Black to move

1...♗a1! (for 1...♗d4? see the next diagram) 2 ♖b4 ♚g7 3 g4 hxg4 4 ♖xg4 ♚h6 5 ♚f7 ♚h5 6 ♖xg6 ♚xh4, with a draw.

6) White to move

2 ♖b4 ♗a1 3 g4 hxg4 4 ♖xg4 ♚h7 5 ♚f7 ♚h6 6 ♖xg6+ ♚h5 7 ♖g1 ♗d4 8 ♖h1 and White wins as 8...♗f2?! runs into 9 ♚f6 ♗xh4+ 10 ♚f5.

99

Queen against Pawn

Winning zones

As the queen is much stronger than the pawn, this ending is only interesting if the pawn is already on its seventh rank. Usually the queen wins even in that case (see diagram 1), but there are two important exceptions: the rook's pawn and the bishop's pawn. Here there is a stalemate defence that can only be broken if the attacking king is nearby. It follows that there are winning zones for the attacking king. Diagram 3 shows the winning zone for a rook's pawn and diagram 4 for the bishop's pawn with the defending king on the 'safe' side (i.e. near the corner square) and diagram 5 with the king on the 'dangerous' side of the pawn. If the attacker's king is inside the zone then he wins if it is his turn to move. If the king is outside the zone, then it is a draw.

Our first position shows the standard case where the queen wins (vs a centre pawn or a knight's pawn). The queen uses a sequence of checks to force the king in front of the pawn; then the attacking king moves in one square and the manoeuvre is repeated until the king is close enough to win the pawn or for the queen to give mate.

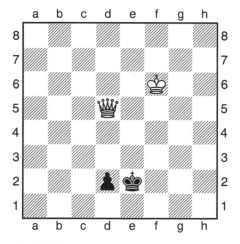

1) White to move

By 1 ♕e4+ ♔f2 2 ♕d3 ♔e1 3 ♕e3+ ♔d1 White forces the black king in front of the pawn. The king takes the opportunity to move in: 4 ♔e5 *(2)*.

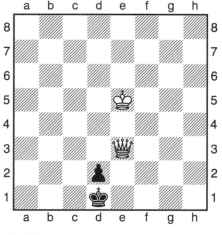

2) Black to move

4...♔c2 5 ♕e2 ♔c1 6 ♕c4+ ♔b2 7 ♕d3 ♔c1 8 ♕c3+ ♔d1 (now the king can come closer once again) 9 ♔e4 ♔e2 10 ♕e3+ ♔d1 11 ♔d3 and White wins.

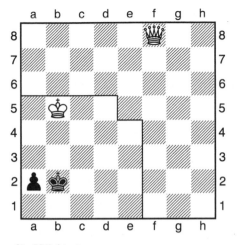

3) White to move

The white king is close enough to win: 1 ♕b4+ ♔c2 2 ♕a3 ♔b1 3 ♕b3+ ♔a1 4 ♕d1+ (not 4 ♔b4?? stalemate) 4...♔b2 5 ♕d2+ ♔b1 6 ♔b4 a1♕ 7 ♔b3 and despite the new-born black queen, White wins.

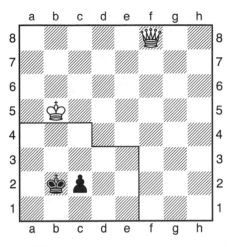

4) White to move

White's king lies outside the winning zone. 1 ♕b4+ ♔a2 2 ♕c3 ♔b1 3 ♕b3+ ♔a1 4 ♕c3+ (4 ♕xc2 is stalemate) 4...♔b1 5 ♕d3 ♔b2 6 ♕e2 ♔a1! and Black holds the draw.

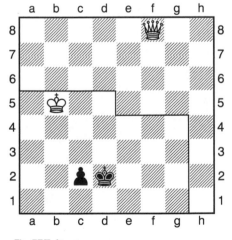

5) White to move

White wins as follows: 1 ♕f4+ ♔d1 2 ♕d4+ ♔e2 3 ♕c3 ♔d1 4 ♕d3+ ♔c1 5 ♔c4 ♔b2 6 ♕d2 ♔b1 7 ♔b3 c1♕ 8 ♕a2#.

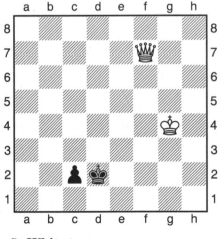

6) White to move

A sample win with the king on g4 runs 1 ♕a2 ♔c3 2 ♕a3+ ♔d2 3 ♕b2 ♔d1 4 ♔f3 c1♕ 5 ♕e2#.

101

46   Queen Endings 1

The drawing zone in the corner furthest away

Queen and pawn vs queen is a very difficult ending as the queen has so many moves, and there are often very lengthy checking sequences. If the defending king is in front of the pawn then the draw is relatively easy. If not then there are two main cases. With a bishop's pawn or a central pawn, the attacker has excellent winning chances – see diagram 4, which is from Matamoros-Bologan, Khanty-Mansiisk 2005. With a rook's or knight's pawn there are drawing zones for the defending king. The most important are in the corner furthest away from the queening square of the pawn. Diagram 1 shows a drawing zone vs a rook's pawn and in diagram 2 (from Negi-Postny, Elsinore 2009) we see a similar zone vs a knight's pawn. The logic is that when the black king is in these regions, there is less scope for crosschecks – i.e. answering a check from the black queen by interposing the white queen and simultaneously giving check to the black king. Finally, diagram 6 (from Mastrovasilis-Shavtvaladze, Athens 2004) shows that friendly pawns can be the defender's undoing as they can prevent checks.

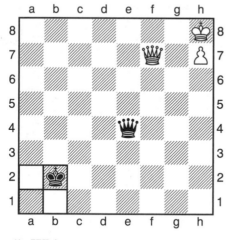

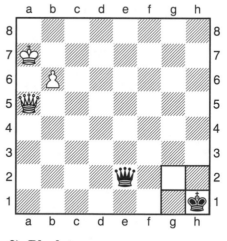

1) White to move

1 ♔g7 (1 ♕g7+ ♔b1 2 ♔g8 ♕e8+ and 1 ♔g8 ♕a8+ 2 ♕f8 ♕d5+ are also drawn) 1...♕g4+ 2 ♔g6 ♕d7+ 3 ♔h6 ♕h3+ 4 ♕h5 ♕e6+ and White cannot make progress.

2) Black to move

The black king is within the drawing zone and with careful defence he can avoid loss: 124...♕f2 125 ♕d5+ ♔g1 126 ♔b7 ♕f8 127 ♕d4+ ♔h1 128 ♕e4+ ♔g1 129 ♕e3+ ♔h1 130 ♔a7 *(3)*.

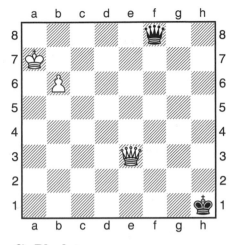

3) Black to move

130...♛f2!? (a typical stalemate motif) 131 ♛e4+ ♚g1 132 ♚b7 ♛f7+ 133 ♚c6 ½-½. Defence in these endings is never simple, but knowing where the king belongs is an excellent start.

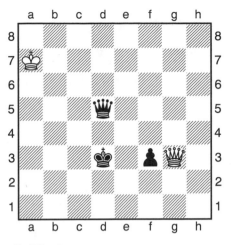

4) Black to move

With a bishop's pawn there is no far-away drawing zone for the defending king. Black wins: 82...♛d4+ 83 ♚a6 ♚e2 84 ♛h3 f2 85 ♛h5+ ♚e1 86 ♛a5+ ♚d1 87 ♛h5+ ♚c2 88 ♛e2+ ♚c3 (5).

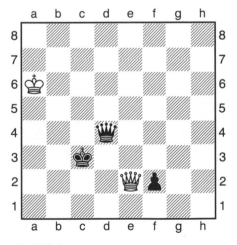

5) White to move

89 ♚b7 ♛g7+ and White resigned due to 90 ♚b8 ♛f8+ 91 ♚b7 ♛f7+ 92 ♚b6 f1♛.

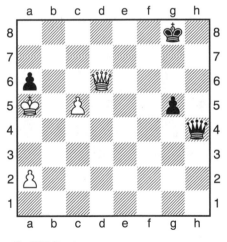

6) White to move

White's c-pawn is further advanced than Black's g-pawn, and this proves decisive: 65 c6 ♛c4 66 ♚b6 ♛b5+ 67 ♚a7 (the king is sheltered by Black's a-pawn) 67...a5 68 ♛b8+ 1-0.

<table>
<tr><td>ENDGAME LESSON</td><td>47</td><td colspan="2"># Queen Endings 2</td></tr>
</table>

Centralize the queen, head for the hills and
create a powerful passed pawn

Queen endings with more pawns can be easier than queen and pawn vs queen as there are more ways to shelter from checks. One important strategy, "head for the hills", was coined by Angus Dunnington in his excellent Gambit book *101 Winning Chess Strategies*. It is a typical way to convert a passed pawn into victory – see diagram 1, which is from Sherzer-I.Almasi, Hungarian Team Ch 1995.

Furthermore, centralizing the queen is often a very important theme – see diagram 3, which is from the game Kovchan-Gershon, Kharkov 2002. A well-advanced passed pawn is a potent force that can outweigh a significant material disadvantage, as can be gathered from diagram 5, which occurred in K.Müller-Lauber, Hamburg 1997. Diagram 6 (from the elite-level game Carlsen-Wang Hao, Stavanger 2013) shows that an attack can arise quickly, as the queen is a mating force in its own right, if supported by just a pawn or two, or the king.

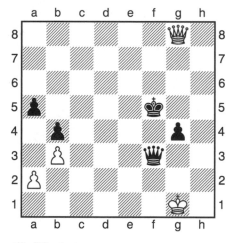

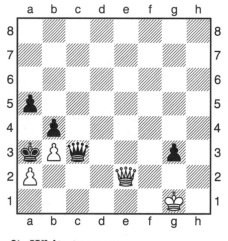

1) Black to move

Without the queenside pawns, this position would be a simple draw. However... 1...g3 2 ♕c8+ ♚e4 3 ♕e6+ ♚d3 4 ♕c4+ ♚d2 5 ♕d4+ ♚c2 6 ♕c5+ ♚b2 7 ♕e5+ ♕c3 8 ♕e2+ ♚a3 *(2)*.

2) White to move

Black's king has arrived in the pawn-shelter. 9 ♕e6 ♕a1+ 10 ♚g2 ♕xa2+ 11 ♚h3 ♕h2+ 12 ♚g4 g2 13 ♚f3 g1♘+ 14 ♚e4 ♕e2+ 15 ♚f5 ♕xe6+ 0-1.

104

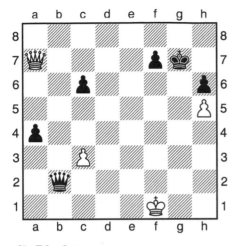

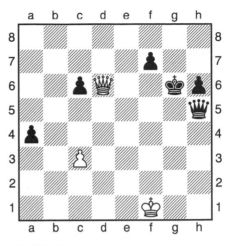

3) Black to move

42...♛c1+ (not 42...a3? 43 ♛d4+, drawing) 43 ♚f2 ♛d2+ 44 ♚f1 ♛f4+ 45 ♚e2 ♛e5+ 46 ♚f1 ♛xh5 47 ♛d4+ (47 ♛xa4 loses to 47...♛b5+) 47...♚g6 48 ♛d6+ *(4)*.

4) Black to move

48...♚h7! 49 ♛xc6 ♛f5+ and White resigned due to 50 ♚g2 ♛g6+ 51 ♛xg6+ ♚xg6 52 c4 a3 and 50 ♚e2 ♛e6+ 51 ♛xe6 fxe6 52 ♚d2 ♚g7.

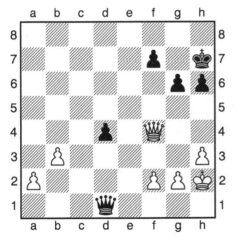

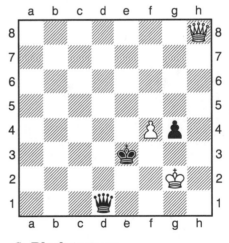

5) Black to move

The d-pawn secures the draw: 31...d3! 32 ♛xf7+ ♚h8 33 ♛f8+ (33 ♛xg6 d2 is also drawn) 33...♚h7 and the game was drawn later.

6) Black to move

76...♛f3+ 77 ♚g1 (77 ♚h2 g3+ 78 ♚g1 ♛f2+ 79 ♚h1 ♛f1#) 77...♛f2+ 78 ♚h1 ♛f1+ 79 ♚h2 g3+ and White resigned due to 80 ♚xg3 ♛g1+ 81 ♚h4 ♛h1+.

48 Queen against Rook (no Pawns)

Break first the third-rank, then the second-rank and finally Philidor's defence

The queen always wins against a lone rook, unless there is an immediate mate, perpetual check or stalemate. The winning nature of the ending has been known for a long time and humans had believed that it was quite easy to win. But the creation of the endgame database in 1978 changed that picture. Against stubborn defence it is very difficult to win within the limits of the 50-move rule. So you should study the winning process in detail:

1) Force the rook back into a third-rank defence.

2) Break the third-rank defence.

3) The defender then usually sets up a second-rank defence. Force the defender into a Philidor win from there. Diagram 3 shows Euwe's way to do it.

4) Win the rook from Philidor's position (see diagram 1).

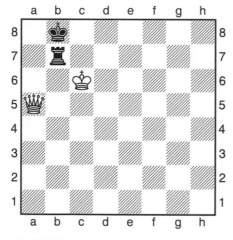

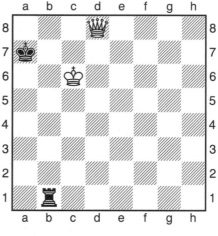

1) White to move

This is the basic winning pattern to aim for. 1 ♕e5+ ♚a8 2 ♕a1+ ♚b8 3 ♕a5 ♖b1 (White wins after 3...♖h7 4 ♕e5+ ♚a8 5 ♕a1+ ♚b8 6 ♕b1+ or 3...♖f7 4 ♕b4+ and now 4...♚a8 5 ♕a3+ or 4...♚c8 5 ♕d6) 4 ♕d8+ ♚a7 *(2)*.

2) White to move

5 ♕d4+ ♚a8 6 ♕h8+ and now 6...♖b8 allows instant mate by 7 ♕a1#, while after 6...♚a7 7 ♕h7+ ♚b8 8 ♕xb1+ White has picked off the rook and mates soon.

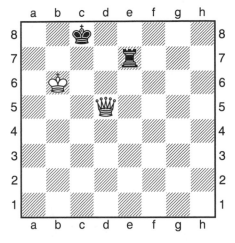

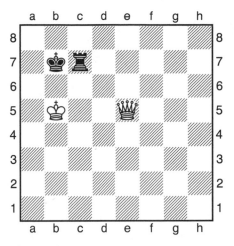

3) White to move

Euwe analysed the following method: 1 ♕f5+ ♚d8 2 ♔c5 ♚c7 (2...♚e8 loses to 3 ♕c8+ ♚f7 4 ♔d6) 3 ♕d5 ♖d7 4 ♕e5+ ♚b7 5 ♔b5 ♖c7 *(4)*.

4) White to move

6 ♕e8 and White wins after 6...♖c1 7 ♕e4+ ♚c8 8 ♔b6 or 6...♚a7 7 ♕e4 ♖b7+ 8 ♔c6 ♚a8 9 ♕d5 ♚a7 10 ♕d8.

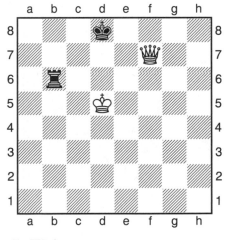

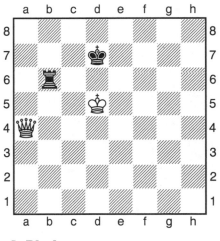

5) White to move

1 ♕f4!? breaks the third-rank defence. The rook has no safe square on its third rank, so the king must make a concession: 1...♚d7 (1...♚e8?! 2 ♕e3+ and 1...♚c8 2 ♔c5 ♖a6 3 ♕c4 ♖f6 4 ♕c3 are both winning for White) 2 ♕a4+ *(6)*.

6) Black to move

2...♚c7 3 ♕a7+ ♚b7 4 ♕c5+ ♚b8 5 ♔d6 ♖g7 6 ♕b4+ ♚b7 7 ♕e4 ♖b6+ 8 ♔c5 ♚a7 9 ♕d4 ♖b7 10 ♔c6+ ♚a8 11 ♕d5 ♚b8 12 ♕a5 and White wins, as we have already seen in diagram 1.

Mate with Bishop and Knight 1

The W-manoeuvre of the knight

This technique is more much difficult than the four basic mates that we saw at the start of the book. Mate can only be forced in a corner, and not just any corner either: it must be one where the bishop can control the corner square itself. Both minor pieces must play a specific role, coordinating precisely with each other.

I have divided the procedure into two lessons; we start with the W-manoeuvre, with which the defending king is forced from a 'wrong' corner into a 'right' corner. The knight must follow a W pattern (as marked in the first diagram), while the bishop makes zugzwang (tempo-losing) and cut-off moves, and the attacking king follows the defending king. The next lesson covers the play leading up to the point where the W-manoeuvre is needed.

We join the action just after the knight has forced the defending king out of the 'wrong' corner square:

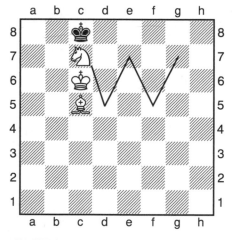
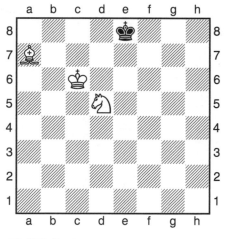

1) White to move

1 ♗a7 (covering b8, so the black king must move away from the 'wrong' corner) 1...♔d8 2 ♘d5 (the first step of the W-manoeuvre) 2...♔e8 (2) (or 2...♔c8 3 ♘e7+ ♔d8 4 ♔d6).

2) White to move

3 ♔d6 ♔f7 (or 3...♔d8 4 ♘e7) 4 ♘e7 (the next step of the W-manoeuvre) 4...♔f6 5 ♗e3 (3) (just in time, the bishop combines with the knight to stop the king breaking free into the open).

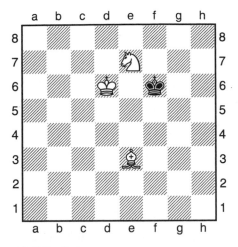

3) Black to move

This is an important position. Black's king cannot escape, and must return to the edge of the board. 5...♔f7 6 ♗d4 ♔e8 7 ♔e6 ♔d8 8 ♗b6+ ♔e8 (4).

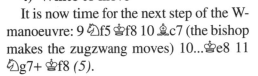

4) White to move

It is now time for the next step of the W-manoeuvre: 9 ♘f5 ♔f8 10 ♗c7 (the bishop makes the zugzwang moves) 10...♔e8 11 ♘g7+ ♔f8 (5).

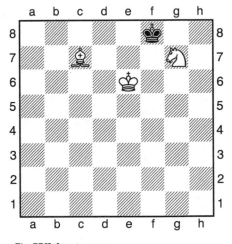

5) White to move

Now White's king and knight imprison Black's king: 12 ♔f6 ♔g8 13 ♔g6 ♔f8 14 ♗d6+ ♔g8 (6).

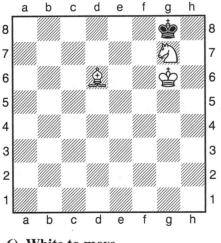

6) White to move

Finally comes the mating phase: 15 ♘f5 ♔h8 16 ♗e7 ♔g8 17 ♘h6+ ♔h8 18 ♗f6#.

50 Mate with Bishop and Knight 2

Use the bishop for zugzwang; the knight rarely moves

The initial phase, in which the defending king is forced into a corner, is not easy to put into one general scheme. I suggest that you play over this example and then practice it against a friend or a computer until you can really master it with the clock ticking. In general it works like this:

1) Bring the king closer.

2) Force the defender back by controlling the squares around the king.

3a) If the defending king heads for a 'wrong' corner then manoeuvre the knight into position for the start of the W-manoeuvre.

3b) It is even better if you can imprison the defending king near a 'right' corner.

This mating technique is quite difficult, especially due to the 50-move rule, but with practice you can get the hang of it.

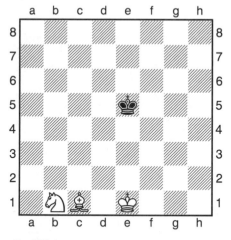

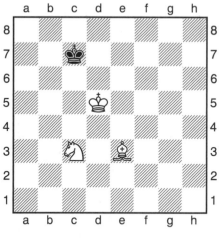

1) White to move

First the king, the slowest piece, moves up: 1 ♔e2 ♔e4 2 ♗e3 ♔d5 3 ♔d3 ♔e5 4 ♘c3 ♔d6 5 ♔e4 ♔c6 6 ♔e5 ♔d7 7 ♔d5 ♔c7 *(2)*.

2) White to move

The knight now heads for c7, one of the starting squares for the W-manoeuvre (see Lesson 49): 8 ♘b5+ ♔d7 *(3)* (for 8...♔b7, when the king heads for the wrong corner, see diagram 6).

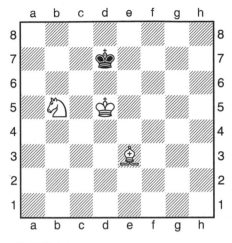

3) White to move

9 ♗f4 ♚e7 10 ♗e5 ♚d7 11 ♘a7 (creating a barrier) 11...♚e7 12 ♘c8+ ♚f7 13 ♚e4 ♚e6 14 ♘b6 (another barrier) 14...♚e7 15 ♚f5 ♚f7 16 ♗f6 ♚e8 17 ♚e6 ♚f8 *(4)*.

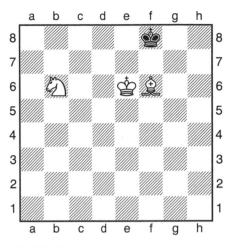

4) White to move

Now a typical path to mate is 18 ♘c4 ♚e8 19 ♘d6+ ♚f8 20 ♚f5 ♚g8 21 ♚g6 ♚f8 22 ♗g5 ♚g8 *(5)*.

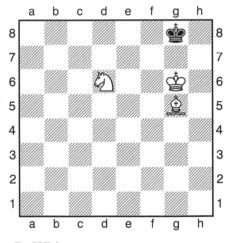

5) White to move

The king is imprisoned in the 'right' corner and mate can finally be delivered: 23 ♗e7 ♚h8 24 ♘f5 ♚g8 25 ♘h6+ ♚h8 26 ♗f6#.

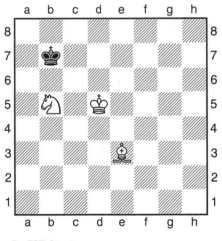

6) White to move

9 ♚c5 ♚b8 10 ♚c6 ♚a8 11 ♘c7+ (only the knight can force the king out of the 'wrong' corner) 11...♚b8 12 ♗c5 ♚c8 and the starting position of the W-manoeuvre is reached (see Lesson 49).

Test Your Endgame Skills

In the following 36 diagrams, your task is indicated below each diagram: in most cases you need to find the winning (or drawing) idea for White.

If you have read the book carefully, you should be able to work out most of the answers. However, some of these exercises are quite difficult, so don't be discouraged if you can't solve them all.

Solutions start on page 119.

Target Scores

If you tackle the tests without using the hints, the number of positions correctly solved corresponds to your endgame ability roughly as follows:

34-36   **Master standard**
28-33   **Excellent club level**
22-27   **Very good endgame skills**
16-21   **Promising endgame ability**
11-15   **You'll impress them at the chess club!**
6-10   **You've learned a lot!**
0-5   **Let's hope you can force checkmate in the middlegame...**

RULE OF THE SQUARE

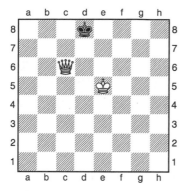

1) White to play and mate in 3 moves
Hint: see Endgame Lesson 1

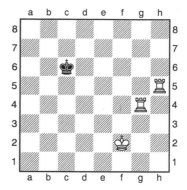

2) White to play and mate in 3 moves
Hint: see Endgame Lesson 2

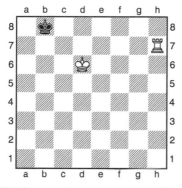

3) White to play and mate in 3 moves
Hint: see Endgame Lesson 4

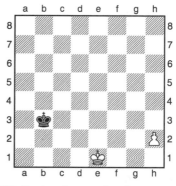

4) White to play and win
Hint: see Endgame Lesson 6

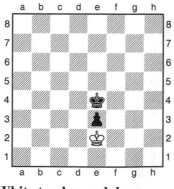

5) White to play and draw
Hint: see Endgame Lesson 7

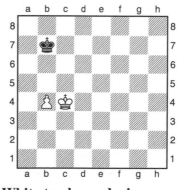

6) White to play and win
Hint: see Endgame Lesson 8

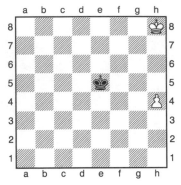

7) White to play and win
Hint: see Endgame Lesson 9

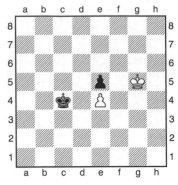

8) White to play and win
Hint: see page 10

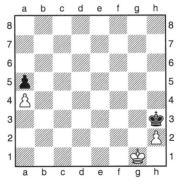

9) White to play and win
Hint: see Endgame Lesson 15

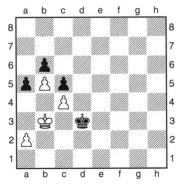

10) White to play and draw
Hint: see Endgame Lesson 16

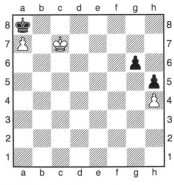

11) White to play and win
Hint: see Endgame Lesson 17

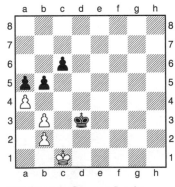

12) White to play and win
Hint: see Endgame Lesson 19

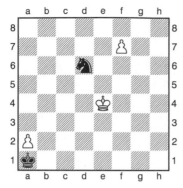

13) White to play and win
Hint: see Endgame Lesson 20

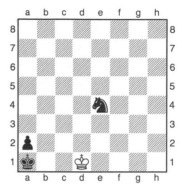

14) White to play and draw
Hint: see Endgame Lesson 21

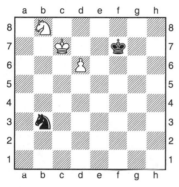

15) White to play and win
Hint: see Endgame Lesson 22

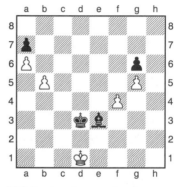

16) White to play and win
Hint: see Endgame Lesson 23

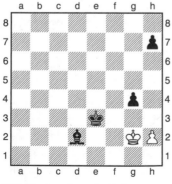

17) White to play and draw
Hint: see Endgame Lesson 24

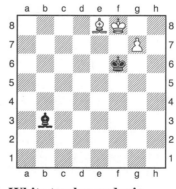

18) White to play and win
Hint: see Endgame Lesson 25

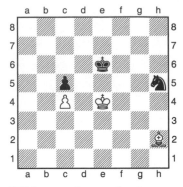

19) White to play and win
Hint: see Endgame Lesson 29

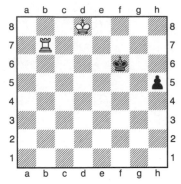

20) White to play and win
Hint: see Endgame Lesson 31

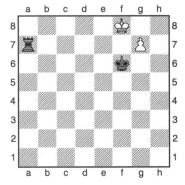

21) White to play and draw
Hint: see Endgame Lesson 31

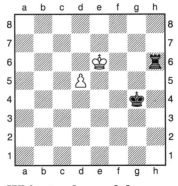

22) White to play and draw
Hint: see Endgame Lesson 31

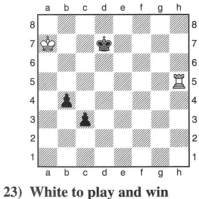

23) White to play and win
Hint: see Endgame Lesson 33

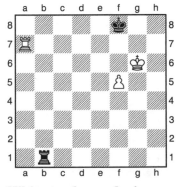

24) White to play and win
Hint: see Endgame Lesson 34

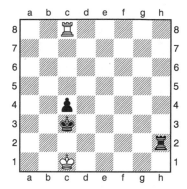

25) White to play and draw
Hint: see Endgame Lesson 34

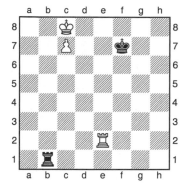

26) White to play and win
Hint: see Endgame Lesson 36

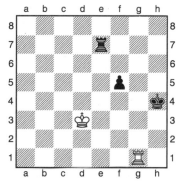

27) White to play and draw
Hint: see Endgame Lesson 37

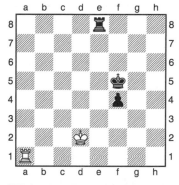

28) White to play and draw
Hint: see Endgame Lesson 37

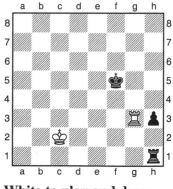

29) White to play and draw
Hint: see Endgame Lesson 38

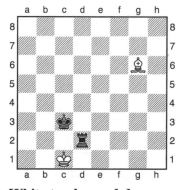

30) White to play and draw
Hint: see Endgame Lesson 43

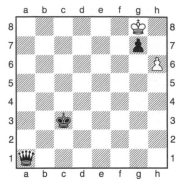

31) White to play and draw

Hint: see Endgame Lesson 45

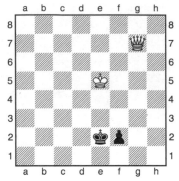

32) White to play and win

Hint: see Endgame Lesson 46

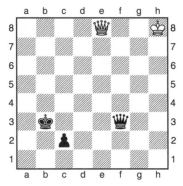

33) White to play and draw

Hint: see Endgame Lesson 46

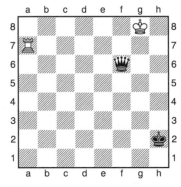

34) White to play and draw

Hint: see Endgame Lesson 48

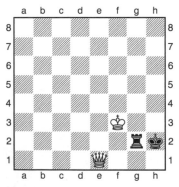

35) How does White (to play) make progress?

Hint: see Endgame Lesson 48

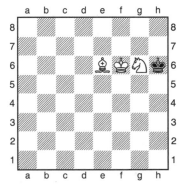

36) Show the first two steps of the 'W' manoeuvre

Hint: see Endgame Lesson 49

Test Solutions

1) 1 ♕b7 (not 1 ♔e6?? stalemate) **1...♔e8 2 ♔e6 ♔f8** (or 2...♔d8 3 ♕d7#) **3 ♕f7#.**

2) 1 ♖g6+ (the lawnmower moves up the board, rank by rank) **1...♔d7 2 ♖h7+ ♔e8 3 ♖g8#.**

3) 1 ♔c6 (the black king is pushed into the corner, where it must then turn around) **1...♔a8** (1...♔c8 2 ♖h8#) **2 ♔b6 ♔b8 3 ♖h8#.**

4) 1 h4!
The black king can't move inside the square of the pawn (h4-d4-d8-h8). 1 ♔d2? is wrong because the black king can now stop the pawn, and the white king isn't in position to block its path: 1...♔c4 2 ♔e3 ♔d5 3 ♔f4 ♔e6 4 ♔g5 ♔f7 5 ♔h6 ♔g8.
1...♔c4 2 h5 ♔d5 3 h6 ♔e6 4 h7 ♔f7 5 h8♕ and White wins.

5) 1 ♔e1!
The king must move directly backwards so that it can take the opposition if the black king advances to d3 or f3. Not 1 ♔d1? ♔d3 2 ♔e1 e2 3 ♔f2 ♔d2.
1...♔d3
Or 1...♔f3 2 ♔f1!.
2 ♔d1! e2+ 3 ♔e1 ♔e3 stalemate

6) 1 ♔b5!
Other moves allow Black to draw: 1 b5? ♔b6; 1 ♔c5? ♔c7! (taking the opposition) 2 b5 ♔b7 3 b6 ♔b8! 4 ♔b5 ♔b7! 5 ♔a5

♔b8 6 ♔a6 ♔a8 7 b7+ ♔b8 8 ♔b6 stalemate.
1...♔a7
For 1...♔b8 2 ♔b6 ♔a8 3 ♔a6 ♔b8 4 b5, see the main line (at move 6).
2 ♔c6 ♔a6 3 b5+ ♔a7 4 ♔c7!
With a knight's pawn, some care is necessary. 4 b6+? only draws because 4...♔a8 5 ♔c7 is stalemate.
4...♔a8 5 ♔b6!
Not 5 b6?? stalemate.
5...♔b8 6 ♔a6 ♔a8
6...♔c7 7 ♔a7 and the white pawn promotes.
7 b6 ♔b8 8 b7 ♔c7 9 ♔a7 and b8♕.

7) 1 ♔g7!
1 ♔g8? also occupies a key square of the h-pawn, but fails to shepherd the pawn home: 1...♔f5 2 h5 ♔g5 draws. 1 h5? ♔f6 2 h6 (2 ♔g8 ♔g5 and the pawn is lost) 2...♔f7 traps the king in front of the pawn and draws.
1...♔f5 2 h5 ♔g5 3 h6 and the pawn queens.

8) 1 ♔f6!
1 ♔f5?? is a horrible mistake, since after 1...♔d4! the mutual zugzwang works against White: his king must move away, and then the black king takes the white pawn and it is the black pawn that queens.
1 ♔g4? is the only other move that doesn't lose, since White scrapes a draw after 1...♔d3 (1...♔d4?? 2 ♔f5!) 2 ♔f3 ♔d4 3 ♔f2 ♔xe4 4 ♔e2!.

119

1...♔d4 2 ♔f5!

White wins the black pawn on e5 and then queens his own pawn.

9) 1 ♔h1!

Bähr's Rule indicates that White wins, but he must first gain some space. Not 1 ♔f2? ♔xh2, when the black king easily gets back in time to stop the white pawn; e.g., 2 ♔e3 ♔g3 3 ♔d4 ♔f4 4 ♔c5 ♔e5 5 ♔b5 ♔d6 6 ♔xa5 ♔c7 7 ♔a6 ♔b8.

1...♔g4 2 ♔g2 ♔h4

2...♔f4 3 ♔f2 ♔e4 4 ♔e2 is also hopeless for Black, since if he takes the a4-pawn, the white h-pawn comfortably wins the race to promote.

3 ♔f3 ♔h3 4 ♔e4 ♔xh2 5 ♔d5 ♔g3 6 ♔c5 ♔f4 7 ♔b5 ♔e5 8 ♔xa5 ♔d6

Threatening to draw by 9...♔c7!.

9 ♔b6 and the a-pawn promotes.

10) 1 a3!

White builds a stalemate cage. Otherwise he loses his c4-pawn and Black queens his own c-pawn: 1 a4? ♔d4 and 2...♔xc4; after 1 ♔a4? ♔xc4 2 a3, 2...♔d3 releases the white king from stalemate.

1...♔d4 2 ♔a4!

Black can never take the c4-pawn without stalemating White, while Black has no other way to make progress. White simply shuffles his king between b3 and a4.

11) 1 ♔b6!

Stalemating the black king and so forcing a fatal advance of the g-pawn. 1 ♔d6? fails to win the pawn ending as the black king gets back just in time: 1...♔xa7 2 ♔e5 ♔b6 3 ♔f6 ♔c6 4 ♔xg6 ♔d6 5 ♔xh5 ♔e7! 6 ♔g6 ♔f8, with a draw.

1...g5 2 hxg5 h4 3 g6 h3 4 g7 h2 5 g8♕#

White not only wins the pawn race, but does so by giving checkmate.

12) 1 b4!

A shocking blow in a position where it looks like White is on the defensive. White creates a decisive passed a-pawn.

1...♔c4

After 1...axb4 2 a5 the a-pawn promotes directly.

2 bxa5 ♔c5 3 b4+! ♔d6 4 axb5 cxb5

This is a hopeless pawn ending for Black, as the key squares of the b5-pawn lie outside the square of the a5-pawn (see Lesson 13).

13) 1 ♔d5!

White moves into the 'knight check shadow'.

1...♘xf7 2 a4

Now White wins as we saw in Lesson 20 (diagram 3): 2...♘d8 3 a5 ♘b7 4 a6 ♘d8 5 a7.

14) 1 ♔c2!

White's only hope of drawing is to shuffle his king between c1 and c2, but he must put the knight 'on the wrong foot'. The point is that only the white king and the black knight will be able to move, and they will both be moving from a light square to a dark square, and vice versa, with every move. White needs to make sure that when it is his turn to move, the black knight can never be covering the *opposite*-coloured square. 1 ♔c1? loses because after 1...♘c3 2 ♔c2 ♘e2 the knight is covering the dark square c1, and so the king must give ground.

1...♘c3 2 ♔c1 ♘e2+

The knight gives check, but this doesn't inconvenience the king at all.

3 ♔c2

Now the knight must move and the king returns to c1. The black king will never escape from its prison on a1.

15) 1 ♘a6!

Fine's Rule (Lesson 22) should have helped you find the win here: "a pawn on its seventh rank wins if it is supported by its king, unless the defender has an immediate draw". By putting his knight on a6, White makes sure that the pawn safely reaches d7. Instead, 1 d7? allows 1...♘c5 2 d8♕ (2 d8♘+ is a clear draw) 2...♘e6+, removing the new queen. 1 ♘d7? ♘d4 2 ♘e5+ ♔e6 3 d7 ♔xe5 4 d8♕ ♘e6+ is also drawn.

1...♘d4 2 d7 ♘e6+ 3 ♔c8

We know that this position is a win, even if we couldn't foresee all the lines where the pawn promotes. But in fact it is quite simple; e.g., 3...♔e7 4 ♘c7 ♔d8 5 ♘d5+.

16) 1 f5!

The idea is to give the bishop major tasks on two different diagonals. 1 b6?? is no good because after 1...♗xb6 2 f5 gxf5 3 g6 ♗d4 the bishop easily deals with the g-pawn.

1...gxf5 2 g6 ♗d4

The bishop is now tied to covering g7.

3 b6! axb6

After 3...♗xb6 4 g7 the g-pawn queens.

4 a7 and White queens the a-pawn.

17) 1 h3!

Forcing a drawn 'bishop and wrong rook's pawn' position. After 1 ♔g3? h5 2 h3 ♗e1+ Black keeps a g-pawn, winning.

1...gxh3+

1...h5 2 hxg4 hxg4 3 ♔g3 eliminates Black's last pawn, drawing.

2 ♔xh3

Or indeed 2 ♔h1. Either way it is a well-known draw, as the white king cannot be removed from the h1-corner.

18) This is a position from Centurini's analysis that we examined in Lesson 25. White has an elegant winning manoeuvre.

1 ♗a4! ♗a2 2 ♗c2

White's gain of time means that he can bring the bishop round to g8.

2...♔g5 3 ♗h7 ♔f6 4 ♗g8 ♗b1 5 ♗d5 ♗h7 6 ♗e4

The black bishop is deflected and the pawn promotes.

19) 1 ♗e5!

This is the only winning move. White prevents the black knight from returning to the play, and so the black king must give ground.

1...♔d7

1...♘f6+ 2 ♗xf6 ♔xf6 3 ♔d5 is a won pawn ending for White.

2 ♔d5

With the black knight frozen, it is a little like a king and pawn ending where the black king lacks access to some crucial squares. For example, 2...♔e7 3 ♔xc5 ♔e6 4 ♔d4 ♔d7 5 ♔d5 ♔e7 6 c5 ♔d7 7 c6+ ♔c8 8 ♔e6 ♔d8 9 c7+ ♔c8 10 ♔d6 and the pawn promotes.

20) 1 ♖b5!

Only the fifth-rank cut-off wins. White will now have all the time in the world to bring in his king and win the black h-pawn.

1 ♖h7? ♔g5 2 ♔e7 ♔g4 3 ♔f6 h4 4 ♔e5 ♔g3 5 ♔e4 h3 6 ♔e3 ♔g2 7 ♖g7+ ♔f1 is a draw.

1...♔g6 2 ♔e7 h4 3 ♔e6 h3

This allows a standard manoeuvre to win the pawn once it is separated from its king:

4 ♖b3 h2 5 ♖h3 and White wins.

21) 1 g8♘+!

Underpromotion to a knight is the only way to draw; after other moves, White is mated or loses his pawn. It would be easy to imagine a player simply resigning in the diagram position, so it is important to remember that you don't *have* to take a queen when you promote a pawn.

22) 1 ♔e5!

A bodycheck saves White. 1 ♔e7? ♔f5 2 d6 ♖h7+ is winning for Black.

1...♔g5 2 d6 ♖h8 3 d7

This will be drawn, as Black will have to give up his rook to stop the pawn.

23) 1 ♖c5!

The rook paralyses the pawns, using the method we saw in Lesson 33 (though some of the details here are a little different, with the kings closer to the pawns). After most other moves, White loses as the pawns run through and promote. If he tries checking from the side with 1 ♖h7+? ♔d6 2 ♖h6+ ♔d5 3 ♖h5+ ♔c4 4 ♖h4+ ♔b3, then he just about scrapes a draw because 5 ♔b6 c2 6 ♔b5 c1♕ 7 ♖xb4+ ♔a2 8 ♖a4+ is a drawn rook vs queen position because the king can't cross the c-file without dropping the queen.

1...♔d6

1...b3 2 ♖xc3 b2 3 ♖b3 and 1...c2 2 ♖xc2 b3 3 ♖b2 both easily win for White.

2 ♔b6

Not 2 ♖c4? ♔d5 3 ♖xb4 c2, with a draw (White must check on the b-file: 4 ♖b5+ ♔d6 5 ♖b6+ ♔d7 6 ♖b7+, etc.).

After 2 ♔b6 Black loses both his pawns in the standard way.

24) 1 ♖a8+! ♔e7 2 f6+

White manages to advance his pawn to the sixth rank without Black getting a chance to start checking from behind.

2...♔e6 3 ♖e8+ ♔d7 4 f7 and the pawn promotes.

25) 1 ♔b1!

This is the 'short-side defence', which we saw in Lesson 34. 1 ♔d1? ♖h1+ 2 ♔e2 ♖c1 is winning for Black.

1...♖h1+ 2 ♔a2 ♖c1

White also survives after 2...♔d3 3 ♔b2.

3 ♖h8 and White holds the position by checking from the side.

26) 1 ♖e4!

I hope you recognized this as a Lucena position. White 'builds a bridge', intending ♔d7 and an eventual interposition by the rook on the fourth rank.

1...♖b2

1...♔f6 2 ♔d7 ♖d1+ 3 ♔c6 is the same.

2 ♔d7 ♖d2+ 3 ♔c6 ♖c2+ 4 ♔d6 ♖d2+

4...♔f6 5 ♖e6+ ♔f7 6 ♖e5 and the rook will interpose on the fifth rank.

5 ♔c5! ♖c2+ 6 ♖c4 promotes the pawn.

27) 1 ♖f1!

Not 1 ♖h1+? ♔g3, when White runs out of checking distance and the black pawn will advance to its fifth rank. It will then prove unstoppable, as Black heads for a Lucena position.

1...Kg4 2 Rg1+ Kh3

Or 2...Kf3 3 Rf1+.

3 Rf1 Re5 4 Kd4!

A vital point; note that the diagram position would have been lost for White if his king had been on d2 instead.

4...Re4+ 5 Kd3 and Black can make no progress.

28) 1 Re1!

White draws by a vitally important defensive resource. Other moves lose since Black is able to get his king in front of the pawn: 1 Rf1? Kg4 2 Rg1+ (it's too late for 2 Re1 Rxe1 3 Kxe1 Kg3 4 Kf1 Kf3) 2...Kf3 3 Rf1+ Kg3 4 Rg1+ Kf2; or 1 Rg1? f3 2 Re1 (2 Rf1 Kf4, etc.) 2...Re4! (intending ...Kf4, etc.) 3 Rxe4 Kxe4 4 Kd1 Kd3 5 Ke1 Ke3 6 Kf1 f2 and the pawn promotes.

1...Rxe1

If the rook moves away from the e-file, then White's king gets in front of the pawn with an easy draw using Philidor's method – see Lesson 34.

2 Kxe1

This is a drawn pawn ending – see Lesson 8.

29) 1 Kb2!

This is the only move to draw. One way to think about it is that White needs to set up the Vančura position, for which his king must be on b2 or a2, and his rook on c3. Another way to see that this move is necessary (even if you have never heard of the Vančura position!) is that Black is

threatening to play 1...h2 2 Rh3 Ra1 3 Rxh2 Ra2+, so White puts his king on b2 to parry this idea. This point is actually a fundamental basis for the Vančura idea.

1...Kf4

1...h2 2 Rh3 is now a safe draw.

2 Rc3!

The other basic point of the Vančura setup is to move the rook so that it can still meet ...h2 with Rh3, but so it can also check the enemy king from the side, and thus deny it any safe haven.

30) 1 Kb1!

Bishop moves lose because the rook can threaten mate while hitting the bishop: 1 Bh7? Rh2; 1 Bf5? Rf2; or 1 Bb1? Rh2.

1...Rb2+

Attacking the bishop achieves little; e.g., 1...Rg2 2 Bf5 Rf2 3 Bh7, etc.

2 Ka1!

Not 2 Kc1? Rg2.

After 2 Ka1!, the king is in the 'safe' corner, and there isn't a great deal of danger for White any more. The bishop can interpose on b1 or a2 if the rook gives check, and stalemate possibilities then come to White's aid.

31) 1 h7!

1 hxg7? loses because a knight's pawn (like a centre pawn) allows a series of checks that force the defending king to block its own pawn; e.g., 1...Qf1 2 Kh7 Qf7 3 Kh8 Qh5+ 4 Kg8 Kd4 5 Kf8 Qf5+ 6 Ke7 Qg6 7 Kf8 Qf6+, and the black king steadily approaches.

1 Kxg7? loses because White's rook's pawn is only on its sixth rank: 1...Qg1+ 2 Kf7 (or 2 Kh8 Qc5 3 Kg7 {3 h7 Qf8#}

3...♕g5+) 2...♕d4 3 ♔g8 ♕d8+ 4 ♔g7 ♕g5+ 5 ♔h7 ♔d4.

1...♕h1

Not 1...g5?? 2 h8♕+, when White even wins!

2 ♔xg7

2 h8♕?? loses to 2...♕xh8+ 3 ♔xh8 g5.

2...♕g2+ 3 ♔h8 with a standard queen vs rook's pawn draw since Black has no time to bring in his king as he must release the stalemated king.

32) 1 ♕g2

The aim is to force the black king to block the pawn and so to bring the white king in one square closer so that when the black king reaches the h1-corner, the stalemate defence can be foiled by giving mate.

1 ♕g4+ is the only other winning move, but it comes to the same thing after 1...♔e1 2 ♕e4+.

1...♔e1

Otherwise ♕f1 wins easily.

2 ♕e4+ ♔d1

Or 2...♔f1 3 ♔f4 ♔g1 4 ♕e3 ♔h1.

3 ♕d3+ ♔e1 4 ♕e3+ ♔f1 5 ♔f4 ♔g2

5...♔g1 6 ♔g3 ♔h1 7 ♕c1+ f1♕ 8 ♕xf1#.

6 ♕e2 ♔g1 7 ♔g3 f1♕ 8 ♕h2#

33) 1 ♕f7+!

White draws thanks to a stalemate idea, showing one reason why the defending king is often best placed in the corner furthest from the pawn in a queen and pawn vs queen ending (assuming it can't safely get in front of the pawn).

1...♕xf7 stalemate

34) 1 ♖h7+!

White just keeps checking on the g- and h-files, and Black can only stop the checks by giving up his queen or putting White in stalemate.

1...♔g3 2 ♖g7+ ♔h4 3 ♖h7+ ♔g5 4 ♖g7+ ♔h6

4...♔f5 5 ♖f7 pins the queen.

5 ♖h7+ ♔g6 6 ♖h6+! ♔xh6 stalemate

35) The basic point is that if it is Black to play in the diagram position, he must make a concession by moving his rook to a more exposed square, which allows the white queen to pick it off with a series of checks. So White transfers the move to Black with a cunning queen manoeuvre.

1 ♕e5+ ♔h1

1...♔g1 2 ♕a1+ ♔h2 3 ♕e1 is 'mission accomplished': we have the starting position but it is Black to move.

2 ♕h8+ ♔g1 3 ♕h4

This is a mirror image of the target position, and works just as well for White. One possible finish is 3...♖g8 4 ♕e1+ ♔h2 5 ♕e5+ ♔h1 6 ♕a1+ ♔h2 (6...♔g1 7 ♕h8#) 7 ♕a2+ and the rook is lost.

36) 1 ♗g8

The knight's 'W' manoeuvre here is g6-e5-g4-e3-g2, the aim being to move the black king into the 'right' h1-corner.

1...♔h5 2 ♘e5 ♔h4

2...♔h6 3 ♘g4+ ♔h5 4 ♔f5 and the king must continue walking towards h1.

3 ♔f5 ♔g3

Or 3...♔h5 4 ♘g4.

4 ♘g4 ♔f3 5 ♗c4

The king is now confined near the corner where it will be mated – which is the purpose of the 'W' manoeuvre.

Sources

Books
Fundamental Chess Endings, Müller and Lamprecht, Gambit 2001
Secrets of Pawn Endings, Müller and Lamprecht, Gambit 2007
How to Play Chess Endgames, Müller and Pajeken, Gambit 2008
Understanding Chess Endgames, Nunn, Gambit 2009
Dvoretsky's Endgame Manual, Dvoretsky, Russell Enterprises 2003

DVDs
Chess Endgames 1-14, Müller, ChessBase Fritztrainer DVDs, Hamburg 2006-13

Periodicals and Magazines
Informator
New in Chess Magazine
ChessBase Magazine and CBM Blog at ChessBase.com
The Week in Chess
Chess Today
Endgame Corner at ChessCafe.com

Databases and Programs
ChessBase Mega Database 2013
Deep Fritz 13
Deep Rybka 4
Houdini 3
Nalimov's 5- and 6-man tablebases
Ken Thompson's 5- and 6-man databases

BODYCHECK

For Further Improvement

1) Refuse draw offers, fight to the end and analyse the games and especially the endgames afterwards.

2) Dive deeper into the magical world of endgames with a standard manual like *Fundamental Chess Endings* by Müller and Lamprecht, Gambit 2001, or *Understanding Chess Endgames* by John Nunn, Gambit 2009.

3) Analyse games of great endgame artists like world champions Capablanca, Karpov, Kramnik and Carlsen.

4) Play endgames from this book against a computer or a friend until you are really sure that you can, e.g., defend the standard draws in the endgame rook vs rook and pawn.

5) Challenge a friend to an endgame competition, which could run like this: both of you study all 50 lessons from this book. Then each can choose four positions to play out against each other.

TRIANGULATION

Did you know...?
You can read the Chess for Kids series on your tablet or phone!

And you don't need a set or board – you can see all the positions and play all the moves just by tapping on the screen. It's like a chess book that has magically come to life.

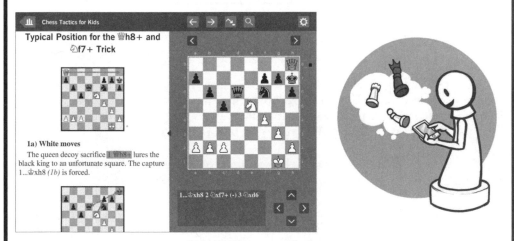

Gambit's Chess Studio app is available for both Android and Apple devices, and is free to download. There's nothing to lose – try before you buy! As well as our kids books, there are well over 50 other Gambit titles available for the app, covering all aspects of chess, and from beginner level right up to books for super-experts. Prices range from $7.99 to $17.99, and once you've bought a book, you can read it on all your compatible devices. You can have a whole chess library in the palm of your hand.

gambitchessstudio.com